AWAKENING ALIVENESS

THE ART OF COHERENT CREATION

ALARA SAGE

Founder of Ecstasia Academy

The information in this book is intended for educational and inspirational purposes only. The author and publisher assume no responsibility for how readers apply the material contained herein.

Published by Vanta House Publishing LLC

ISBN: Paperback: 979-8-9959317-1-3

Hardcover 979-8-9959317-0-6

eBook: 979-8-9959317-2-0

awakeningaliveness.com

Printed in the United States of America

A Note on the Text

The client stories shared throughout this book are composite illustrations drawn from years of working with hundreds of people. Names and identifying details have been changed to protect privacy. They are offered in service of the teaching, not as accounts of specific individuals.

For Nana

Thank you for seeing my light long before I knew I had one. Thank you for speaking the prophecy of this book into existence, into my ten-year-old ears, so that I could carry it with me until its birth.

CONTENTS

*Aliveness awakens where
separation is met.*

INTRODUCTION

I remember the moment my body dropped to the ground after watching my bank account drain to zero. Multiple six figures, stolen right out from underneath me.

Moments ago, my life appeared perfect. I was proud of what I had built. The business, the purpose, the partner who adored me, and two loving and healthy boys. I had checked every box of success. If there had been a ribbon to award, I would have been first in line to receive it.

Money was flowing.

But underneath that flow was a hum. Like the soft wind in the night that constantly brushed up against my window. Never allowing me to fully rest.

I was unfulfilled.

Internally, I was separated from my wholeness. And from that separation, an identity of not enough was born. A wound so deeply painful that, although I was aware of it, I chose not to meet it. I chose not to feel it. I chose to deny myself its presence.

Instead, I plastered a smile on my face whenever someone looked my way. I wore the mask of holding it all together. It felt like sandpaper against my skin. But I chose the sandpaper over the truth. Because the truth felt more unbearable than the friction.

And still, it was insatiable. Hungry beyond measure.

I was sitting in the living room of a temporary house in Irvine, California. My boys were at the pool with my partner, Danny. The house was quiet. I had been working with a mentor, a man referred to me by a friend, a man I trusted, helping me invest in crypto. That afternoon, I was on my phone with him and on my computer managing the accounts when my heart dropped as my bank account went to zero.

I turned to my phone. But our entire conversation had been deleted instantly. Every message. Gone. I messaged him immediately, thinking it was some kind of glitch.

He pretended not to know me.

Despite weeks of conversation, he became an absolute stranger in a single second. I felt powerless. Betrayed. Shame washed over me like a cold, wet towel. It left me paralyzed in shock and fear as the full weight of it landed in my body. Like having the breath ripped from your lungs. And even as you grasp to regain your composure, your body refuses to respond. You try to breathe, but your lungs won't open to draw the air back in.

I was a single mother. I was responsible for more than just myself. How could I have let this happen?

I felt like a failure. Like a fool who had been conned, and I was not the type of person to be conned. I wanted to crawl into a hole and forget about everything.

Then the voice of my Higher Self cut through. Reminding me of my innate capacity to create my desires. My body immediately shifted its energy from low and hopeless to courageous.

As a little girl, I would spend hours in my imagination, living and breathing my desires into existence. At age seven, I desired a horse more than breathing. I obsessed over it, drew horses, played horse, and within a few years, I somehow got my first horse. I had no idea how powerful this was until years later.

All throughout my life, family and friends recognized something in me. "You always get what you want," they would say. Some with admiration, some with frustration. Since it was a natural talent, I didn't recognize it as something special.

So in that moment, sitting on the floor in the ice-cold clutch of fear, I breathed. Deep into my body. And slowly, conviction replaced the fear. "I've created it once. I'll create it again."

I picked myself up off the floor and vowed to make all the money back again. The conviction was real. And the shock was still moving through my body like a current I couldn't stop.

I don't remember walking to the pool. Like a zombie, I moved through the house to where my partner, Danny, and my boys were. Their laughter filled the air, bright and oblivious. It felt like the universe was mocking me. I stood there with a dry mouth, trying to find the words. As if saying them made it real. Maybe if I never said them, it would remain a dream.

Danny's face went blank when I told him. He is a protector by nature, and the blankness turned quickly to anger, for me, on my behalf. Like he was going to track this man down and do something about it. But I knew he couldn't. I knew there was nothing to be done.

The money was gone.

In the six months that followed, I didn't make it back as I had vowed. Instead, my business collapsed completely.

Clients left. Launches stopped selling. It was as if someone had switched the light off.

I realized that I hadn't been using my own teachings. The hum that had been there before was still present. It wasn't a desire; it was an addiction. An addiction that was born from the identity of "not enough," and it had overtaken my life.

My intuition had warned me over and over again. I had heard the faint mention of it in the background of the noise. But I kept choosing the noise.

Watching my business collapse finally stopped me dead in my tracks. I had been trying to fill a hole that was never meant to be filled, only met.

And what a pill that was to swallow. The minute I truly acknowledged this in myself was the moment I came face-to-face with the identity that had caused me all of my suffering.

All the rejection. All the failure. All the moments that still plagued me in my sleep. The girls in school who didn't like me simply for existing. And rather than standing in my own truth, I withered. I shrank away as if they were holding some knowledge about me that I wasn't privy to. As if their rejection was the verdict.

This one belief. This one identity that I had allowed to create my reality. And that was just the beginning. It wasn't the end. It wasn't the moment of transcendence. It was the moment of the trench. The moment I finally looked around and realized how deep a hole I had truly dug for myself.

Now, even here, we would all love to hear how I was able to "heal" the wound of unworthiness and quickly regain my footing. But that is not the story I am here to tell.

I did not regain my footing easily. And this book is the result of that. Because I took all the hard roads. I took the road of "healing." I took the road of "changing" myself. I continued, over and over, to choose the roads that only validated the very thing I was working so diligently to "fix."

Everything I did further emphasized the identity of "not enough."

You know that hum. The not enough that lives underneath everything you've built, everything you've achieved, everything you've done. You may have never named it. But you've felt it. In the quiet moments between the doing. In the numbness that settles when you stop long enough to feel. In the faint sense that no matter how much you accomplish, something essential remains just out of reach.

That is where this book begins.

Did I ever recognize my wholeness and remember who I truly was? Yes, I did. It came in moments, standing in the shower, heart blown open by the sheer depth of what the wound had taught me. Tears streamed down my face as gratitude rippled through my chest. I wept in honor of it. I wept at the epiphany of the many layers of truth it slowly revealed from within me. That beneath every failure, every rejection, every moment of not enough, I had never actually been any of it. The ground beneath all of it had never moved. My greatest pain became my grace.

So let me help you avoid the suffering that brought me here. This book will show you how to create your reality without fueling the wound of separation.

It doesn't try to change you. It meets you.

This book meets you as the creator. It anchors you back into wholeness. From there, from that place of worth and sovereignty, you create your reality—coherently.

PART ONE
THE FOUNDATION OF AWAKENING

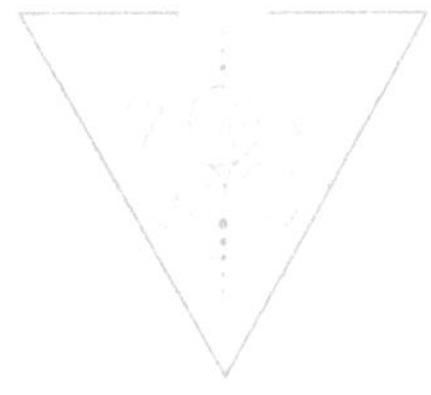

CHAPTER I

CREATOR CONSCIOUSNESS

In 2014, I was driving my car down a back road in the mountains of Colorado, headed to work on my first horse of the day. I was an equine physical therapist.

Shortly after leaving home, I heard my Higher Self say to me, "Om three times."

At this point in my life, I was meditating regularly. I had spent years studying yoga deeply. I was on a spiritual journey, so I knew what "Oming" was, but I didn't personally practice it.

Still, I listened to my Higher Self and took a deep breath into my body. I slowly toned "OM" until my breath reached its end. The low vibration filled my car like a bugle calling to something ancient. The sound bounced off the sides and back in on itself, like a small orchestra. I repeated it two more times, each one deeper, fuller, more alive.

At the end of the third breath, a visceral and intense energy shot from the base of my body, through my center, and up and out of my head, like a ball of lightning moving through me in a single split second. I went into a full-body orgasm.

I had never experienced a full-body orgasm. I pulled the car over and allowed myself to be fully present to the waves of ecstasy that coursed through my body. It was like an orgasm on steroids. Every single cell of my physical body, and every single photon of my subtle bodies, resonating at the highest level of bliss possible.

It went on for several minutes. Slowly, I came down. Everything had shifted. The light outside the car looked brighter. The air around me was buzzing as if I could feel each individual atom. It felt surreal and simultaneously deeply alive and grounded. The joy that remained in my body was unlike anything I had ever felt.

I had absolutely no idea what had just happened to me. I had never experienced anything even close to this moment.

I was lit. Alive!

I turned my car back onto the road and headed for the freeway. But the energy in my body had no interest in simply driving.

I cranked the radio on, started singing at the top of my lungs, and dancing in my seat. Probably not the safest thing to do when you are speeding down the freeway, but bliss doesn't live in logic or fear, and it certainly wasn't entertaining either.

That day I worked on several horses. They dropped into a trance quicker and deeper than ever before, constantly licking and yawning as they released. I wasn't doing anything different. I had simply shown up with a different energy.

After that, my experience was far from blissful. I still had no idea what had happened to me. But over the next five months, I experienced the full spectrum of human emotion. Despite not knowing what was going on, I could sense the emotions that I had stuffed down or denied were coming to the surface in full fury.

Honestly, I had always thought of myself as grounded, relaxed, and emotionally stable. But the truth I experienced firsthand was that I had actually been very emotionally shut down, not emotionally stable.

It was pure chaos.

One minute, I would be laughing hysterically. The kind of laughter that makes you think you've lost your mind. Then, the next minute, I would be on the floor in pure grief. Floored by sorrow. Moments later, I would be raging and trying to tear down the walls of my house.

I was a new mother. My son was an infant. In these moments, I felt overpowered by a part of me that I clearly did not know. There were moments I felt guilty for the self-centered experience I was having. I wasn't always available to his needs. But I didn't feel like I was in control. The top had been blown off, and I couldn't stuff it all back inside anymore.

Several times throughout the experience, I asked my Higher Self if I was going crazy. The only answer I ever received was, "breathe and allow."

Five months. Every emotion under the sun. And only then did I find out what had happened to me. Magically, a book landed in my lap, called *Kundalini Awakening*. I don't even remember how I received the book.

In this book, the first chapter talks about spontaneous kundalini awakenings. It described the exact experience of what I had just been through, almost to a T. The bliss, the emotions, and even the potential for psychosis. When I read that word, I felt it land in my body. I had bordered on the very edge of clinical insanity. I knew that with every cell of my being.

The relief of finally having answers. I cried. I screamed. It was as if a sick joke had been played on me. But of course, it hadn't. Instead, it was the beginning of the most powerful transformation of my life.

What the Awakening Revealed

From this experience, one thing became clear. I was living a lie. And not only that, I was living a shut-down, half-lived existence. The awakening made me realize how numb and dissociated I truly was.

Over the years of sharing this story, a client who was struggling to orgasm once said to me, "Well, it was easy for you. You had the awakening, and from then on, you lived in orgasm."

So let me be clear. That is far from what happened.

Did I begin to experience full-body orgasms after that day? Yes, but I also experienced all of my sexual trauma with full force.

Did I begin to feel more alive in life? Yes, but I also noticed the deep oppression within myself even more clearly.

Just like the story of the money, this experience wasn't the finish line. It was the beginning of an intimate connection to my body, my creative energy, and what turned out to be my incredible capacity for Aliveness.

The experience blew me open, no doubt about that. I started to connect to a wisdom within me that I couldn't explain. I would give talks, and people would say, "That's Buddhism" or "That's Tantra." But I hadn't studied any of these. Things would come out of my mouth that I had never heard before.

My Higher Self was reminding me of what I had always known. Creator Consciousness. The full spectrum from Fragmented Creation to Coherent Creation to Ecstatic Creation.

But the information, the wisdom, still was not the full story. I then went on to experience all of it. That is the story of the money, and so many other stories, that I tell throughout this book.

Because conceptual knowledge is great, but experience is where that knowledge becomes lived Aliveness. And I'm gifted with the ability to channel wisdom, but that doesn't make me exempt from having to learn through the challenges that life brings.

And in fact, it is the lived experience that makes the teaching real.

Coherent Creation is the ability to create your reality from a place of worthiness and sovereignty, where Aliveness awakens. Before my awakening, I was creating from fragmentation. Separation. Even though I had been on a spiritual journey for several years, practiced intense yoga, breathing, and meditation, the illusion of separation was still the one running the show.

I was becoming more aware of this. But my spontaneous awakening opened my eyes to the deeper truth.

As I mentioned in the introduction, I have spent years healing myself. Shifting my identity and countless other modalities that only strengthened the underlying wound of not enough.

That wound comes from one source: the belief that we are separate from Creation, Source, God, Love. This wound is the core of human suffering. Give me any belief, any perceived limitation, and I will show you how it leads back to this one single belief.

At its core, that wound breeds shame. The lowest vibratory emotion. Diabolical by nature. Not enough is the face that shame wears in the everyday. Recognizable. Familiar. Almost comfortable in its constancy.

And from this wound, the perpetual friction of duality attempting to reunite, Fragmented Creation is born.

Fragmented Creation is the absence of awareness, embodiment, and surrendered action. In this wound, the ego attempts to fill what cannot be filled. Like the crater left by a comet, the impact is real, the hole is vast, and the ego will do anything to fill it.

This filling takes two primary forms.

The first is reactive. It looks like drive and ambition: the workaholic, the overgiving mother, the achiever who always needs just a little bit more. The carrot dangles. You give more, push harder, and the carrot moves further away. The stick that holds it maintains the distance. No matter how much is accomplished, there is always a sense of unfulfillment. Always a sense of not enough.

This is consumerism at its core: the attempt to consume from the external, from the physical reality, in order to fill the void. As soon as I have. As soon as I manifest. As soon as I get. Then I will have arrived. But arrival never comes. Because the ego, the identity, can never be creation itself. It can never fill the void.

The second expression is suppression. The pain of the wound becomes too much to feel, so this person goes numb. They deny their internal desires and shut down to some degree or another. They may have a successful career, a full life on the outside, but their ambition has been quietly directed toward suppressing the self. Suppressing what they say, how they act, their deepest yearnings and desires.

In this suppression, the pure expression of creation cannot actualize into physical form. And therefore, the experience of not enough is always felt.

Both expressions, the reactive and the suppressive, share the same intention. To do whatever it takes to not feel the wound of separation. Two different strategies. The same experience.

Fragmented Creation fuels the external, not the internal. And therefore it will never grant you what you truly desire. You will have moments of climax, real experiences of reaching a goal, of temporary satisfaction, but they will be short-lived. Because the insatiable craving to merge, to live as oneness, cannot be satiated until you learn to meet it.

This is why consumerism consumes without end. Information, experiences, things. Consumption is part of creation, but it is not the full picture. When we unconsciously consume experiences created from lack, we digest lack. We receive lack. When we consciously consume energy and experiences that nourish us, that come from wholeness, we are nourished at a cellular level.

What Aliveness Actually Is

When you consciously consume and create, those two sides stop fighting and come together. Something is released. The Aliveness that was compressed inside the tension of that conflict begins to move again.

It feels like coming home. A home that nourishes you from within. Not just safe. Expansive, free, and attuned to life.

This is Aliveness.

Not an emotion, not a peak experience.
Aliveness is the light of God, the I AM state, shining through every cell, every photon, every atom of your being. The physical body, being the densest form, is the vessel through which Aliveness is lived. You experience Aliveness in your body, not your mind.

You can conceptualize Aliveness. Understand it via your mind. But to live it is to embody it at a cellular level. It is actually a very intense sensation because to reverberate light through physical form requires holding the paradox of creation: the simultaneous truth of separation and unity, form and formlessness, density and light. That is what is asked of the physical body. And where the cells hold the illusion of separation, the belief that they are not that light of God, they deny themselves the very light they are made of.

In the felt sense, Aliveness is communion—and ultimately unification—with Creation itself. It is the feeling you have when you are with someone whom you love and who loves you deeply. The feeling of being seen, accepted, and received exactly as you are. Not as a concept. As felt truth.

Here, at this point of communion, creation ignites. Like the spark of the sperm entering the egg.

Coherent Creation takes you to the belief of separation and meets you there. It reminds you that you are the Creator. Not in some distant, unreachable way, but as a direct fractal of Creation itself. You contain the whole. And therefore, you are One with the Whole and the Whole is One with you.

Oneness.

My dog, Kona, taught me this. Not through her life as a dog, but the minute her Soul returned to her Indigo body.

She was the most extraordinary dog I had ever met. Every single person who met her fell deeply in love with her. She lived to be sixteen.

In 2021, my partner Danny and I were preparing to leave Colorado. She was in a great deal of pain by then, sleeping most of the day.

Years earlier, I had worked as an animal communicator. That ability never left me.

I asked her if she wanted to come with us. I showed her the journey ahead and explained everything. She decided she wanted to be let go from the physical. Part of me was relieved, as I couldn't bear to watch her suffer through the journey. And part of me was immediately aware of the hole her absence would leave.

In my years as an animal communicator, I have witnessed the beautiful relationship animals have with death. Dogs especially taught me this. Once their quality of life was gone, they stayed mainly for their family. So I honored her.

Days later, I sat there on the floor with her while the vet prepared the injection. I looked at her old body, a remnant of who she used to be. She looked up at me. Her eyes steady. She knew what was happening, and she felt calm and safe.

I placed my hands on her and gently whispered beneath my breath the sounds and words that my heart desired to share. I felt that she needed the space to be filled with love, not loss, so I stayed focused on supporting her transition. My eyes were dry. Not a single tear fell in that moment. The vet injected her, and with one last breath, she was gone.

It all felt a bit surreal. Grief always takes me a moment to express.

On the drive home, a heaviness sat between us. The silence of something that had just left the world. And then, almost instantly, her spirit came into my space. I felt her immediately. Joy and love, pure and unmistakable. She began to thank me for everything I had ever done for her. Such honest, complete gratitude, as if I had been extraordinary, when I had simply loved her. I wept deeply as she expressed this. My heart broke open with love and ached with loss simultaneously.

She told me how much she loved me and how much she loved Danny, who had only just met her. She thanked both of us. She thanked him for his kindness and the moments he cared for her in my absence.

Back home, I resumed my packing, but Kona stayed with me. Her spirit wrapped around me like a warm blanket. She was with me for about an hour when I heard what sounded like a male voice say, "She has to go now."

The male voice came from behind my right shoulder, not physical, but unmistakable. My body turned before my mind could question it. As soon as I did that, a flood of Indigo light filled my physical eyes and my mind's eye.

I had heard of this. That when we die, we return to our Indigo body. I was witnessing Kona being reunited with Soul. Pure bliss flooded my body. Very much like the full-body orgasm that day in the car.

But this was coming from Kona. I knew this was her gift to me. To remind me of this Aliveness, even in death. In that moment, there was no pain, no identity, no separation. Just the light of what she truly was, what we all truly are.

I watched it. I felt it move through my entire body as if I were swimming in a warm ocean of light.

It is something I will never forget.

That is what is possible. You as Oneness. Whole. Alive. That is what Coherent Creation, and even more so Ecstatic Creation, anchors you in.

Creation speaks in threes.

The Trinity. The beautiful dance of creation into form. There are infinite expressions of the Trinity of Creation. Even though we often work with them separately, they themselves are not separate.

The Trinity is the Masculine, the Feminine, and the Child. The Masculine and the Feminine are the two poles of creation. They are already drawn toward each other. That magnetism is the nature of polarity itself. But polarity alone does not create. Without the Child, the Masculine and the Feminine remain in friction and conflict, seeking union but unable to find it.

The Feminine is the dark. Not darkness as absence or wrongness, but darkness as infinite creative potential. She is the void, the womb, the vast field of everything that exists before form. She contains all of it, unactivated, waiting. She is the yearning. The magnetic pull of creation toward itself. Her pure expression is total availability to feeling, to sensation, to being met by life without flinching. I am the yearning.

The Masculine is the light. The spark. The precise, directive intelligence that pierces the dark and activates it. Like the sperm entering the egg, that single point of contact where potential becomes creation. His pure expression is the sovereign vision that sees not just what is possible, but how it comes together. How energy moves into form. How the formless becomes actual. I am the architect.

That friction is the illusion of separation, duality expressing itself. And it is also, paradoxically, the creative force that drives the seeking.

It is not something you achieve.
It is what you have always been.

The Child is the coherence. The pure love that holds both without collapsing into either. In its presence, the interference of opposition falls away. And separation unifies.

The Child is a paradox. It exists before polarity, as Spirit exists before mind and body. And yet it is also what is remembered when the polarity merges. When light meets dark, the Child is not created. The Child is remembered. This is not a problem to solve. It is the nature of innocence itself. I am innocence.

This is where the Trinity meets. And where the Trinity meets, Creation arises. Not from effort. Not from force. But from pure existence. Beneath every identity, every belief, every story you have ever told about yourself, there is a presence that has never changed. That is the I AM.

Your physical body is not separate from the I AM. It is held within it, like Russian dolls nested inside each other, each one contained within something larger, all of it one. The I AM—the Great Causal Body—is the largest, containing all others: the causal body, the subtle body, and the physical body.

In the I AM, everything already exists. Every desire, every expression, every timeline you feel called to live, is already held within that body. Complete. Whole. Coherent Creation is not the act of making something from nothing. It is the act of remembering what already is, and allowing it to actualize into physical form.

Creation moves from that presence, the I AM, beingness, isness, into form via your beliefs, emotions, and actions. In Coherent Creation, we learn to remember ourselves as it.

It is not something you achieve. It is what you have always been. The illusion of separation creates the experience of having left it. And therefore the feeling of not-enoughness. The incomplete. The inadequate. Coherent Creation is the practice of recognizing that you can never not be it.

Every time you anchor your awareness in the I AM state, you allow the pure existence of Creation itself to shine through you, unobstructed. Here, the Trinity merges. And from that merger, wholeness is realized. Oneness. Beingness. Existence. Creation.

Within Coherent Creation, we learn to create from that space through three pillars: Awareness, Embodiment, and Action. These are the Trinity actualizing into form through you. The Child, the Feminine, and the Masculine moving through the human experience of creation. Each pillar has its pure expression and its shadow.

Awareness is the expression of the Child. Its pure state is the innocent witness, a neutral presence to what is, the capacity to love and accept without preference, without siding. The loving observer who sees without judgment. Its repressive shadow is withdrawal, the observer gone silent, presence collapsed into absence. Its reactive shadow is judgment, criticism, right versus wrong, and at its most contracted, shame. The innocent observer turning against what it sees.

Embodiment is the expression of the Feminine. Its pure state is total availability to feeling, the body as a vessel of truth, fully present to sensation, open to being met. Its repressive shadow is numbness, dissociation, stagnation, the Feminine shut down, and feeling denied. Its reactive shadow is sensation-seeking, craving, performing, feeling, using the body to consume or to be seen rather than to arrive.

Action is the expression of the Masculine. Its pure state is movement that arises naturally from clarity, from what is innate in the moment, from what lights the Soul without effort, from the sovereign vision that trusts its own knowing. Its repressive shadow is paralysis, the Masculine collapsed, unable to move. Its reactive shadow is control, efforting, doing in order to get, the architect forcing what wants to flow.

These three pillars are not separate from the body. They live in you as Three Creator Centers: the heart, the sacral, and the Third Eye. The Child in the heart. The Feminine in the sacral. The Masculine in the Third Eye. One system. Three expressions. You will meet each of them fully in the chapters ahead. But they are already within you. They have always been within you.

The wound of separation is forgetting. The Child forgotten. The Feminine shuts down or is chaotic. The Masculine forcing or controlling. Coherent Creation is the condition under which remembering happens.

To remember, we must hold the I AM and meet what arises. Here, the three aspects of the Trinity merge back into Oneness. Singularity. And Aliveness is awakened. The Trinity of Creation is a living intelligence that continuously returns you to yourself.

For years, the teachings that have been spread throughout humanity on this topic have not held the complete picture. And so, they have not worked.

Coherent Creation is not simply about thinking something into existence. It is not simply about thinking positively or being "high vibe." The mind is a wonderful tool, but when filled with programming of lack, it becomes its own destructive force.

Think of the mind like a computer. It knows what you program into it. When we are young children, we become programmed by our parents, guardians, and environment. Much is learned by watching, not by direct teaching.

When I was a little girl, I became shy and withdrawn because the world around me didn't feel safe. My parents would tell me they were fine even though I could feel that they were not. My teachers would pretend to be happy when, instead, I could feel a deep sorrow within them. When I tried to express or voice this dissonance, I was told that I was wrong. I began to distrust the wisdom of my body and my own intuition. It felt like confusion. A strong sensation in my body, undeniable and real, being told it wasn't there.

These early years don't just create beliefs. They create separation within us. Parts of our psyche split off, carrying the weight of what wasn't safe to feel or express. These parts operate from the subconscious, disconnected from our wholeness. They aren't broken. They aren't wrong. They are simply waiting to be met.

And the work of Coherent Creation, through presence, awareness, and embodiment, is learning to meet them. Not to fix them. Not to remove them. But to include them back into the wholeness that was never actually lost.

Animals are another mirror of this internal separation. When I was an animal communicator, I quickly learned that the problems rarely originated from the animal itself. Unbeknownst to the owner, they were programming the animal with their own vibrations.

Animals showed me how their owners, carrying their own unmet fear and lack of safety, would be leading them on a leash, telling them, "Everything is okay, stay calm." But animals aren't listening to the words. They are feeling the emotions of the human.

The dog ends up acting aggressively because it is mirroring its owner.

The dog's aggression then triggers the owner even more within their own tension, and the cycle is validated and anchored more into the physical reality. The dog isn't responding to who the owner thinks they are. They are responding to the tension caused by the internal separation of Self.

Where duality meets, God is revealed.
Where duality is met, Aliveness awakens.

This is why embodiment is paramount to Coherent Creation. Being positive or thinking good thoughts sounds nice, but it doesn't create results. You have to be willing to meet yourself within every single moment of creation.

To feel the full experience. This is communion. This is the art of creation. It isn't about just the highs or even the results. It is about who you are when the experience of separation is screaming from the cells within your body. When your ego desperately desires to fill the void.

Can you meet yourself in that pain? Can you meet yourself there as wholeness? That is the depth of Coherent Creation. It is truly the mastery of being the Creator. Creation doesn't deny itself its failures. It lives with them, in them, as them.

It allows them, no matter how much of an eyesore they are. Because Creation doesn't judge them as such, it doesn't deem them unfit or ugly. It deems them simply an expression of creation. Meeting yourself in your body, in the breath, in life, when your ego wants to deny you the experience. That is Coherent Creation.

Creation is perfection. Not perfect in some ideological way. Perfect, as in, if it exists, it is a necessary part of the whole. That can be challenging sometimes to understand. It can be painful to experience. But the truth remains.

When you learn to meet the pain in your body from a state of wholeness, you no longer identify with the pain. It simply is. It exists just as pleasure exists. The existence of both sides of the coin is creation. Where duality meets, God is revealed. Where duality is met, Aliveness awakens. Creation stops being something that you reach for, and returns to your natural, innate beingness.

Sometimes understanding something from what it is not clarifies what it is. Coherent Creation is not here to heal you. It is not here to upgrade you. It is not manifestation.

Coherent Creation works by reminding you that you are not your wounds, not your identity, and although you do create your reality, it actually isn't through visualization and affirmations.

I spent years in all the above with varying results. What I love about Coherent Creation is that it anchors you into Truth—the I AM. When you anchor into Truth, creation is inevitable, and Aliveness awakens.

In 1999, I was a senior in high school. Despite being a top student and always being driven, by the time I hit my senior year, I had no idea what I wanted to "be". At that time, computers were the future, and I was told that if I became a computer programmer, I would definitely be successful.

I truly enjoyed computers. I still do, despite my deeply mystical and esoteric self. So I thought, great, I'll do that.

I told my mother that I wanted to go to DeVry Institute of Technology and become a computer programmer. She stared at me with a completely blank face, and after a few very long seconds, she said, "Are you sure that is what you want to do?"

Looking back, she knew me far better than I knew myself. A tomboy at heart, always outside riding horses bareback in the rain, computers, sure.

But I had my sights set. So I went about studying for the SAT, and despite being a talented student, I scored ten points below the minimum entry requirement.

Three times. Three times I took the test and scored the same. By the third time, I came home and fell on the ground, exhausted. I started to bawl my eyes out.

My mother looked at me again and, this time, very tenderly said, "Are you sure that this is what you want to do?"

Out of nowhere, I said, "No, I want to travel the world." I had no idea that I held that desire. But as soon as those words left my mouth, my entire body lit up with the truth of it. Something in me had been waiting for that moment.

And from that declaration of my desire, everything in my reality shifted very quickly to create it.

I had no money. I was a high school kid with a big dream. So I picked up two more jobs. Working from 4:30 a.m. until 11 p.m., straight from one to the next. No social life, no spare time. Every ounce of my being was focused, directed on my desire. Despite the long hours, I wasn't exhausted. I was alive.

Everything aligned. There was action, but no effort. I was creating from a state of wholeness, desire, focus, and pure joy.

After six months, I had the money I needed. At nineteen, I boarded my first flight ever and flew to Fiji. A new chapter had begun.

I created that entire experience without visualization or affirmations. I had never heard of either. I didn't know what any of it would look like. I simply said yes to what was true, and then I moved.

Years later, that understanding deepened when I began working with clients. Many of them struggled to visualize the life they desired. Not because they lacked imagination, but because they were working from lack instead of being anchored in truth. You cannot visualize your way out of an identity of not enough.

If visualization comes naturally to you and feels effortless, do it. But if you have to force it, it isn't power. It's force. And that is not Coherent Creation.

Coherent Creation is art. In art, creation flows through you. You are the vessel that structures the beautiful light of God into form. Any artist, no matter what medium, who has tried to effort in creating knows that the results are always subpar at best. It isn't the expression of the Genius. It is the expression of the ego/mind attempting to force creation.

The distinction is drastic. And once you feel it, you will know when you are in which state. The practice is the awareness of that state, and inviting yourself back into the I AM state over and over again. Like a wave that builds until the conditions are met, and then it breaks onto the shore, completing its creation. Not forced. Not mental. Simply inevitable.

When It All Comes Together

Once I realized my desire to travel the world, the Feminine aspect was established. She worked internally to cultivate that desire, the yearning to receive, to be met by creation. The Masculine went about focused, directional, carrying out the action needed to earn the money, organizing the trip, and planning. He took her creative life force energy and turned it into action.

The Child remained in a state of innocence, awe, and curiosity. I wasn't trying to force anything. I was holding the state of joy, and from that coherence, the Feminine and Masculine merged with the Child.

In Coherent Creation, you remember yourself as the I AM state. The state of pure existence, isness, creation. From that state, each aspect of the Trinity moves from that purity. In the I AM, what you desire already exists in your most subtle field. Instantly. And from that purity, you create. That quality actualizes into form via your beliefs, emotions, and actions. Naturally. Worthy, Sovereign, and Alive.

The I AM is the source. And therefore, when you are in that state, you are everything that you could ever be. Nothing is lacking. Nothing is not created. From that state, creation becomes fluid. The idea that you have to effort in order to create comes from the state of separation, duality.

Of course, you have to take action. But taking action and efforting are not the same thing. From the state of I AM, all of that is clear. Even the most challenging of actions is experienced as fluidity instead of force.

This is how you create your reality beyond your ego mind. Beyond duality. Because when you only create from duality, it is Fragmented Creation. Duality creates duality. It, in and of itself, is not enough, not whole, not complete. What is missing is the Child, not the inner child of healing work, but the Child as the coherence that allows the Trinity to merge. Without it, the Masculine and the Feminine remain in friction, and creation remains fragmented and dualistic.

In duality, you create both sides, attempting to find the point of creation, the unification. You might create abundance in one aspect of your life only to create lack in another. This opposition seeks to meet itself and awaken Aliveness from within. The natural homeostasis of creation will always seek to unify.

You have always sought this unification. With yourself, with others, with creation. This very core human trait is the beautiful expression of Coherent Creation. There is ultimately nothing outside of yourself that can ever grant you this unification, this fulfillment. Learning to Coherently Create isn't just about creating your desires. It is about fulfilling the core human desire to unify with Source. To realize yourself as the I AM presence.

To live from that state of joy, magnetism, and sovereignty.

The I AM

Take a moment to bring your awareness to your physical body. Feel your breath move rhythmically in and out of your body. Now, in your mind or out loud, state, "I AM". And continue to simply observe your body.

Notice what arises. Notice what you feel. Imagine every single cell of your physical body letting the light of God shine through it. Like the lens of a projector. Breathe and feel this. Notice where in your body expands naturally. Notice where in your body contracts. No judgment; simply allow your body to respond exactly as it does.

Breathe and allow. Repeat the statement, "I AM," over again. Feel the truth of this statement resonate through your cells. Feel the remembrance. The authenticity of this statement and the experience of the state.

State it again: "I AM". And breathe more. Each time you state this, let it inform your physical body. Allow the truth of the statement to be. Existence. Consciousness. Beingness.

When you feel complete, come out of the moment and write down what you experienced. Practice this daily. Practice it alone in a quiet place and then, when you feel ready, begin to practice it, even for a moment, around other people, in busy environments. State it inside your mind and allow it to inform your body of the Light of God emanating from every cell. What do you observe?

Allow yourself this precious gift. Learn to meet yourself at the moment separation arises. In that moment, Aliveness awakens.

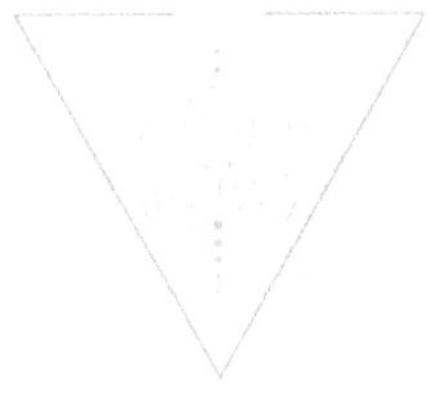

CHAPTER 2

SOUL'S COMPASS

My client, I'll call her Tracey, had a life she was proud of. Yet none of it lit her up.

She was a well-respected and successful lawyer with decades of work under her belt. She had built a career that anyone would admire. She was living the life that made sense. She always had a warm laugh that made everyone smile. But inside, she didn't feel like something was missing. She felt like something was hiding.

When I first asked her what she desired, there was a pause. Her mouth opened as if to answer, only to close again. Her face held the look of someone searching for something just out of their awareness, like a word on the tip of your tongue.

But no clear desire revealed itself. Not from her heart, anyway. Yes, she could name some goals and express some ideas. But she didn't feel connected to any of them.

Instead of desire, what arrived was its opposite. She didn't desire to hide anymore. She didn't desire to keep suppressing something that she yearned for, but could no longer name.

In that moment, the absence was the answer. Because what Tracey was pointing to wasn't a goal or a dream. It was the part of her that had never actually left. Only been forgotten.

The truth was, Tracey had been shut down early in life by her family. They had judged her and shamed the innocent exploratory nature of her own body.

Something that happens to many of us.

In a moment of play, our hands explore our bodies only to find and experience pleasure. A warmth, a connection to something that feels true and alive within us. But then we are caught and scolded. A devastating shock that ends up living in our bodies as unresolved trauma and feeds the separation of self from within.

For Tracey, this became the belief that she was unsafe being herself. So she had donned the identity of her family. Their world. Their profession. Her childhood had felt like a stream of mishaps that somehow separated her from her family. Her heart naturally pulled her toward them, and yet she felt as if there was a hand that kept her at arm's reach. Distant and different.

This beautiful desire to be included, received, and accepted is something that often pulls us from our worthy, sovereign, and alive selves.

But Tracey didn't come to me broken or suffering. She was content, successful, and enjoying her life. But she was not alive. She knew this the minute we connected to it. It was like a dull gray that lightly covered her reality. She saw and felt the colors of living, but the vibrancy was muted ever so slightly.

It is easy to simply move through life in a state of contentment. When nothing is truly wrong, that comfort often doesn't create enough friction to inspire change.

But Tracey was courageous and willing. During our time working together, she retired early at the age of sixty-five and began to pursue what truly lit her up, listening for the first time to the Aliveness within.

One day, she sent me a voice note. I could feel the smile in her voice as she gave a little chuckle, "It feels like it's all coming together to create a life where I nurture and simultaneously get nurtured. It's truly beautiful. I don't know what shifted, but I am embodying me."

Her Core Desire had been to experience her own brilliance. Not brilliance from the mind or the ego, but the light of her heart.

Tracey's story is the revelation of creation from seed to fruit.

Your Soul Is Speaking

Desire is the seed of creation. In it is the entire "code" required for its full expression, much like a fruit tree seed contains everything needed to move from germination to bearing fruit.

The misunderstandings surrounding desire are many. In many spiritual and religious teachings, desire is labeled as sinful or as "of the flesh" and something that should be avoided completely.

But desire is not only a natural aspect of the human experience; it also holds the great wisdom of our Soul within it.

Desires, when clear, come from the Soul. They are the breadcrumbs that our Soul gives us to help us remember what we came here to learn and experience. They are not wrong or bad, and when understood, they become a glorious part of your journey.

Core desires are not ego wants. The ego focuses on what it can get or experience in the external reality as a form of separation from the Self. Whereas Core Desires exist to bring us back to parts of ourselves that we deeply seek to meet and understand. In that moment of reunion, we awaken the Aliveness that has been dormant within.

Desire is about one thing, and one thing only—unification.

Every single why behind a desire will point back to this if you follow the trail far enough. The desire for wealth has nothing to do with money. It is the desire to experience abundance, freedom, and security. To feel, without a single doubt, that you are always provided for. That resources, opportunities, and support arrive at the perfect time. That you would never want or lack.

Take a moment to feel into that. The experience of complete provision. From that knowing, there is no need to hoard, to save, to grip. Saving money when it comes from fear is actually an expression of distrust. A very human experience, and one I don't want to brush past. We don't trust ourselves or Source because of the wound of separation. From that distrust, we feel we must have reserves. We must have extras. But if unification were experienced within, if wholeness were remembered, that entire need would dissolve.

Every desire, at its root, is the Soul's
longing to come home.

The same is true of love. It is natural, deeply human, to desire companionship. Someone to share life with, to co-create. But the pain of seeking that experience in another, only to find that they too believe in separation, has caused extraordinary suffering. When unification is found within, that need is no longer projected onto the relationship. And paradoxically, this grants the relationship permission to be fully human. To hold imperfection, tension, and conflict as part of its learning, rather than as evidence of its failure.

The desire for purpose follows the same trail. We desire to be part of something larger than ourselves. To give back. To be seen and known for something of legacy. This is ultimately the desire to create from oneness, for oneness. To bring your genius forward in service of the whole.

Every desire, at its root, is the Soul's longing to come home.

And this is where something essential must be understood. Physical reality is duality. It is always two. The person and the thing desired. The self and the other. Subject and object, forever distinct, forever reaching toward one another but never collapsing into one. Even when you get the thing, the money, the love, the recognition, there remains a you and an it. Duality, by its nature, cannot deliver what only wholeness can.

Think of the atom. A proton and an electron generate enormous energy between them. Positive and negative, charge and orbit, pull and push. But without the neutron, the atom is unstable. It cannot hold its form. It flies apart. The neutron is the stabilizing principle. Neutral, still, the quiet center that allows the whole structure to cohere.

The Trinity works the same way. The Father is direction, will, the animating force. The Mother is receptive, magnetic, the creative field. And the Child is the coherence, the neutral third, the pure love that holds both without collapsing into either. Without the Child, the Father and the Mother are just charges and orbit. Beautiful, powerful, and unstable.

Duality is the atom without its neutron. It generates energy, but it cannot sustain a unified form. And this is precisely why the external world, which is always duality, cannot fully grant you your desires. Because the third principle, the stabilizing coherence, exists only within you, as you.

The external can reflect unification. It can even catalyze it. But it cannot be it.

This is why every desire is ultimately pointing inward. The Soul is not confused when it desires. It is precise. It is pointing you, always, back to the I AM. Back to the pure existence, beingness within where unification is not sought, but remembered.

Your desires show you exactly where the I AM has not yet been felt as lived truth. That is the invitation. And the meeting of that invitation is where creation arises. Naturally. From the wholeness of what you already are.

Every single time you choose to come back to that point, where separation screams at you to chase the external, and you meet yourself there, you awaken Aliveness within. Your desires are the compass back to this point. Over and over again.

Are You Chasing or Hiding?

And from this understanding, we can see the three relationships a human can have with desire.

The first is the reactive—pursuing desire from lack. The second is the repressive—denying desire from lack. The third is creation—meeting desire from wholeness.

Through the lens of separation, we experience lack. And lack attempts to actualize desires in two ways. The first is through the reactive nature. This is when desire is pursued as a means of acquiring. It often looks like ambition from an external viewpoint. Here, the lack drives the identity from underneath, saying, "I am not enough until I have this."

The reactive relationship to desire feels like an insatiable appetite to achieve. It holds the tension of anxiety within the nervous system, like a tightly drawn bow ready to fire. A goal is reached, a climax hit, but it leaves before you are even granted the pleasure of its enjoyment. Pleasure is not a lived experience in the reactive state. It passes through before it can be felt.

The second lens is the repressive nature. This is the denial of the desire altogether. A suppression of its existence and a subconscious avoidance of feeling it. Here, lack drives it from the identity of "I am not enough to have this."

The repressive relationship feels like numbness. Like desiring to curl up in a blanket on a cold winter day with no desire to go outside and face the cold. You pull back from people, from experiences, from life itself. Afraid to live. But the fear is rarely felt. The oppression has deadened the feeling of it. Pleasure here is hard to even touch. Like it is always just beneath the surface, unable to be reached.

When we learn to meet our desires within, we integrate the separation. From this wholeness, the desire is created in full brilliance. No performance, no doing in order to get, and no numbing of its truth. Here, the creation is pure. Authentic. Alive.

Meeting desire from wholeness feels alive. It is a state of flow where the impulse to create moves through you like a dance. Like that song that causes your body to move without any instruction from the mind. No thought. No effort. Pleasure pulsating in every cell. Wave after wave, seemingly with no ceiling to its intensity. So intense, in fact, that it requires a great deal of presence to hold it.

The subtlety is in knowing when a desire is a true desire versus one that sounds beautiful or makes sense but doesn't actually feel alive from within. Or one that scares you into suppression.

For instance, I don't have a deep desire to have a community garden, even though I think that is a brilliant idea. I love it. I love plants and Mother Gaia. The idea of it is beautiful. But I don't have any desire to create one. I don't even have any deep desire to necessarily be a part of one. So I could easily say that it's not meant for me in this life. And that is clean.

But if I deeply desired to create one, and even though it overwhelmed me with fear, I did it anyway. I chose to believe that my desires are for me. I recognized that it is only fear masquerading as "it's not meant for me." Then I am owning my desires. And that is clean.

Now, the beautiful truth about repression and reaction is that when they are fully embodied, without a whisper of anything else, they become themselves: Ecstatic Creation.

Repression, which I have experienced very intimately, is so powerful. It can even be spiritual. Sacred Purity. The priest. The nun. The spiritual purist who doesn't allow themselves any desire. Who doesn't care about food, money, partnership, status, or even purpose. The purist lives for only one thing: devotion to God within. That is a profound act. It is the extreme of denial, and it becomes sacred.

Purity in the totality of denial. Because when you deny yourself of everything you desire, you face the longing very, very deeply. You are longing. And the longing transforms from longing for the desire into the longing for God. The longing for Source. The longing for Self.

Reaction lives on the other side of that pendulum: the person who insists on actualizing every single desire and creates magnificent results in life. For that person, every single desire that they feel, they actualize. This is also sacred.

The actualization of desire is not wrong or bad or less than. It is the carrying out of desire into form. And when someone fully surrenders to the impulse of Aliveness from within, taking action regardless of fear, always holding spaciousness for the desire and feeling it in the body, they are immersed in the energy of longing just as the purist is.

This is Ecstatic Creation.

In Ecstatic Creation, you learn to be in a completely surrendered state to the desires and Aliveness from within. Coherent Creation teaches you to create stability for that level of energy by reminding you of your wholeness, where creative life force energy flows freely.

And that stability is not built once. It is chosen, again and again, in the moments when the wound rises loudest. This is an act of devotion. The natural action of love toward yourself and toward what you desire.

Every time the wound of not enough rises and begs you to forget. To chase, to deny, to perform. Devotion is the act of the heart that pulls you back. Back into the moment. Back into wholeness. Back into the truth of what you are.

There will be times when nothing appears to be happening. When the desire feels distant, and the ground beneath you is uncertain. When it looks, from the outside, like failure. These are the moments devotion carries you. Because in those moments, nothing else will support you. Not technique. Not willpower. Not understanding.

Only the remembrance.

The remembrance that you are the I AM. That you can never not be worthy, sovereign, and alive. Devotion is simply this. Returning to that truth, again and again, no matter what the external reflects. It carries you when the gap between what is and what you desire feels widest.

This is felt in the creations that are more challenging to actualize. You know the one. The desire you have worked on, prayed over, released and returned to, and still it mocks you. While other areas of your life flow with relative ease, this one remains untouched. Unchanged. Immovable.

*Your hardest to create desire is your
most sacred invitation.*

The One That Won't Budge

The desires that feel furthest away are pointing to the most solidified identity with separation in your field. The deepest wound. The place where the belief of not enough has its strongest grip on your identity. This is why some people create wealth with ease and cannot create love. Why others draw love effortlessly and cannot create financial freedom. The area of greatest resistance is not where you are weakest. It is where the wound of separation is most entrenched.

Your hardest to create desire is your most sacred invitation.

It is not asking you to try harder, believe more, or surrender better. It is showing you exactly where the core identity structure is holding the illusion of separation most tightly. The desire that feels impossible is the one with the most precise coordinates. The one pointing directly to what your Soul most desires to meet.

Because the truth is, even though I speak to creating your desires, you are doing something far more precise and yet effortless. You are simply holding the truth of the I AM while being fully present to the place within you that has not yet felt that as lived truth. Both simultaneously. The wholeness and the wound. The already-realized state and the separation that contradicts it.

That simultaneity creates a vacuum.

The I AM is the only truth. Within the I AM is the fulfilled desire. Already. Complete. From that state, Creation has no choice but to resolve any contradiction to that truth.

This is why it works. Not because you believed hard enough or held the vision long enough. Because you are only available to the truth. And from that truth, you are willing to meet the pain of the illusion of separation. That is the creative act. The desire does not need to be chased or earned. It needs to be met.

Your desire was never pointing to an external want. It was pointing to a wound your Soul deeply desires to meet.

When you meet it fully, from wholeness, you embody the wisdom that was always held within it. Then the desire can actualize effortlessly into physical form because nothing is denying its truth.

There are three primary reasons people do not create what they desire.

The first is denial. They are in denial that they have the desires they have, or they are in denial that they are worthy of those desires. That the desires are for them, directly from their Soul. Sometimes people secretly crave something, but tell themselves that whatever it is, it is for other people. Not them.

Denial is powerful because it places the truth outside of your awareness. You dissociate from it. This is primarily a protective measure because it hurts to look at. But denying yourself your desires suppresses your Aliveness. It dampens your life and holds you in a state of suppression. Denial doesn't protect you from desire. It only separates you from its Aliveness.

The second reason is that creating your desires will often result in challenges. This is by design. Your desires are not randomly assigned. They point precisely to the places within you where the wound of separation is most entrenched. And the challenges that arise in the process of creating them are not obstacles. They are the meeting points. Each one is an invitation to hold the I AM while facing what contradicts it. The friction is not in the way of creation. It is the creative act itself.

It isn't always easy. You will feel frustrated, angry, or even hopeless some days. But when you can recognize that the challenge is pointing somewhere specific, to a belief, a wound, a place where Aliveness is waiting to be freed, it changes your relationship to it. You stop trying to get through it and start meeting it. And sometimes, in that meeting, suffering becomes grace.

The third reason is the need for control. Initially, I didn't see myself as a very controlling person. But my Higher Self told me that I was attempting to control the outcome of my creations and thus significantly weakening my attempts and delaying the entire process. That made my ears perk up.

Control can be subtle. It is the need for an outcome to look a particular way, show up in a particular fashion, or fulfill itself in a particular timeline. All created from the ego mind that cannot see the bigger picture.

What control actually does is kill magic and kill Aliveness. Because it is the expression of separation. It is saying that you don't believe you are Creation and therefore you have to take it into your own hands, the hands of the ego mind.

Control creates frustration, confusion, and the feeling that things aren't moving. In these moments, step back. Or, better yet, step away. Give your creation spaciousness. The truth is that what desires to be created will be, if you allow it. Sometimes you are so attached to the what, how, and when that you cannot even see how much you are controlling it.

Step back and let your desire speak to you. You will hear it, and it will feel like fluidity in your body.

Learning to release the outcome is the beginning of something that deepens in Ecstatic Creation. The art of surrender, where releasing becomes the creative act itself.

Let Yourself Ache

One day, I was heading out on the trail for a run. I often receive downloads and epiphanies during my time in Gaia.

Just as my shoes hit the path, the Great Mother dropped in. Her energy, familiar and warm in my field, matched the external beauty of the sun's rays through the trees. She had come to teach me about the power of yearning.

She went on to tell me that when we allow the womb to yearn for our desires, it magnetizes the resources needed to create them.

But I was confused. It landed against everything I had taught. The future self. The already-realized state. The practices I had personally shared with hundreds of clients. Was I wrong? Had I been teaching something incomplete?

How could the ache of yearning, something that felt anything but whole, create anything at all? I felt the friction of it in my body. The tension of the mind attempting to logically grasp what wisdom was preparing to show me.

Instead of answering me, she told me to drop into my womb. And so, as I jogged down the beautiful tree-lined trail, I focused my breath and dropped my awareness into my womb.

My womb immediately lit up with Aliveness as my energy began flowing to it. I could see the rose-gold light circling from within. The energetic field of my womb expanded, as did my entire pelvis. The blood shifted in my body, and I grounded deeper into the moment.

She told me to think of something I deeply desired. I paused for a moment, allowing a desire to naturally arise instead of filling the blank with my mind.

Within a second, the desire to be seen revealed itself. The excitement and the fear appearing simultaneously, two sides of the same coin. Then she told me to let myself feel the womb's natural yearning for that desire. I breathed deeper into my womb and, using my intention, brought the desire into it.

As I did this, a great ache swept over my womb. Not sharp, but diffused and deeply intense, the way the body feels when it cramps for menstruation. I was weeks away from my bleed, and yet there it was. Like my womb was longing the way we long in the heart when we miss someone. I had to focus on my breath.

The sensation was almost overpowering.

The Mother told me to stay here and meet myself in this longing. The ache increased. I breathed into it, consciously softening my body, surrendering to the sensation rather than bracing against it.

The most beautiful experience arose. Ripples of love and bliss exploded from within. I could see the complete fulfillment of this desire. Not from my mind, but the actual fulfillment. I saw myself seen, received by large crowds. I felt the sensations in my body of being received by a group of people I deeply cared about. Their eyes filled with love, their arms reaching out to hold me.

My heart burst open, and my whole body went into orgasm. Soft tears escaped my eyes. I had to stop and catch my breath because I wasn't anticipating any of it.

The nurturing voice of the Mother grounded me in the moment. She told me that desire is the fulfilled state. It contains all of it: the idea, the longing, and the fulfillment. Sometimes desires only need to be met. Afterward, the desire dissolves as its journey is complete. Other times, the desire moves all the way through actualization and into the physical.

Not all desires are meant to be actualized into physical reality. This is nature. Look at Gaia; some seeds never germinate. Some sprouts never live to be plants. Some animals are born and then quickly pass away.

Humans often think this is incomplete. That life ended too soon. But nothing in Creation is random. It all holds purpose.

That morning on the trail changed how I understood and thus worked with desire.

The Great Mother taught me the power of surrendering into that longing. That is actually where the magic is. Because as soon as you say, "It'll happen if it wants to," you are evading the longing. Or if you force the creation to happen on your timeline, you are equally evading it.

Longing is uncomfortable.

We know that feeling through grief. When someone we love dies, we long for their presence, knowing we cannot have it. We will never feel their physical body in our space again. That is longing in its rawest form. That is why grief is such a living, breathing, visceral experience for humans. Because we resist it. Because we reject the pain of longing rather than surrendering into it.

Not because longing suggests that we don't have. It is our not-havingness, our not-enoughness, our internal lack that experiences longing as absence. But when we experience longing from a state of wholeness, it is the natural magnetism of the Feminine.

The natural magnetism of creation.

It is the ache of the womb to be filled by creation. When you are connected to your womb or hara, that ache is literal. Like a gentle wave of menstrual cramps. Subtle, soft, but present and insistent. That insistence is the Feminine beckoning. She is calling. Like the siren on the rocks, she draws creation toward her through the sheer power of her longing. Not by chasing. By being so fully herself that creation cannot help but meet her in her yearning.

And that yearning is not magnetizing the desire itself. It is magnetizing the resources through which that desire is created.

When longing is experienced as lack, it is because we are seeing it through the lens of lack. The longing itself is not the problem. The perspective is. And from that perspective, we either chase the desire to make the longing stop, or we dismiss it entirely, telling ourselves it will happen if it's meant to.

Inadequacy lives in that yearning. And so does your aliveness.

The shift happens when you let yourself feel the longing. You meet the longing for what it is. She sings powerfully and viscerally from within your womb. But you have to feel it. You have to meet yourself as the I AM. Whole. Present. Undiminished by the wanting.

You have to become so intimate with it. And as you do, notice what arises. Any level of I don't have. Any level of I'm not good enough. Any level of inadequacy. Because that is exactly where that wound lives.

Inadequacy lives in that yearning. And so does your Aliveness, bound by the fragmentation of the wound of separation. When you meet the inadequacy, you meet the Aliveness.

That is the beautiful truth of it.

But you only see yearning for what it is when you have the courage to feel it over and over and over again. Without needing it to leave your body and become something in the physical, without needing to make it real just to escape the feeling. Because that is the state of force, not creation.

Learning to surrender to the longing is a deep teaching that requires a great deal of stability and presence. It is truly part of Ecstatic Creation. Here in Coherent Creation, I grant you this awareness because I believe that when we understand the full spectrum, each step lands more precisely.

For you, in this moment, the journey starts here, in granting yourself permission to feel your desire.

If you feel nothing, you are not broken. You are not without desire. You are numb. Shut down. And that numbness is not an absence of desire. It is a measure of how much of you is caught in the belief that you are inadequate of such a desire. That you are not enough to have it. The deeper the shutdown, the deeper the desire. And the more potent the inadequacy that screams the wound of separation. This is the chasing and denying cycle.

Chasing and then letting go and dismissing. Feeling the yearning for it, pursuing it, but then denying yourself of it. An internal push and pull that sends you in circles. And this is duality serving its purpose. Because that is where we find the point of creation, where duality meets and Creation is revealed.

This creation point is why we all deeply desire love. The ache to be so close to another that sometimes you don't even know where you end and they begin. And then other times, you relish in your autonomy, you relish in your sovereignty. You dance in that merger of where you come together as unified and where you come together as one. Sovereign, individualized, unique. Duality meeting itself as Oneness.

When you understand your desires as a compass rather than a destination, it creates freedom. You no longer have to make it happen. You can learn to meet your desires in the fullness of their story and allow their Aliveness to reveal the journey.

A client, Laura, and I explored this point within her.

Laura came to me knowing she had a desire, but not yet knowing what it truly was. On the surface, she believed her desire was to share human design, a modality that had lit her up for years.

But as we sat together and I listened to her field, it became clear that human design was the modality, not the desire. So I asked her, "What is the desire?"

Her answer arrived with goosebumps.

"To empower women," she said, "to just be. To exist. Not to hide." And then she paused. Because she recognized it immediately, this was her own journey too.

As we went deeper, the true desire began to reveal itself. To be received. To be accepted. To be seen for her differences rather than rejected for them. Because Laura thinks differently. She always has. She sees patterns where others see chaos, consequences where others see only the moment.

As a child and into adulthood, this gift made her the killjoy in the room. The one who saw what was coming and named it, only to watch the faces of those around her drop.

Her genius had caused her pain. And from that pain, she had made a decision. It is not worth it. She stopped speaking up. She went quiet. She hid.

When those words landed, "It is not worth it," I could feel them hit her heart. Because underneath them was something far deeper than social rejection. It was abandonment. Her own abandonment of herself.

Her pattern recognition, the very genius that makes her extraordinary, had become a construct of control. If she could see what was going to happen, she felt safe. The unknown, the chaos, the wild feminine energy of not knowing, that terrified her. So she used her mind to project patterns into moments, pulling herself out of the present and into a future that didn't yet exist.

But chaos, I told her, is not the enemy of pattern recognition. It is its source. The most extraordinary networks, neurons, mycelium, and the synapses of the brain, are not linear. They are chaotic and precise simultaneously. That is where her genius truly lies. Not in predicting the pattern. In holding the chaos while the pattern reveals itself.

Her desire was never really about human design. It was about network. About seeing how people, each carrying their own Unique Genius, could be woven together into something that hums with collective Aliveness. A living, breathing network where everyone fires from the truth of who they are.

And underneath all of it, the desire to stop abandoning herself. To stand by her own weirdness. To make an internal promise that no matter what, she has her own back.

This is the process of meeting yourself in your desires. Laura stayed with me as we started at the superficial level and together explored the depths of emotion, memories, and truth that desired to breathe into the moment.

We paused often, granting the moment space. I named what was in the field, and together we felt it without requiring it to change, move, or be different. Meeting her desire from the I AM state. By the end, Laura was deeply aware of her Core Desire and knew how to move forward with clarity.

Something had shifted that I could both see and feel. A knowing had returned to her, one that had always been there but slightly misdirected, turned away from its own source. Now it was oriented. Her energy moved freely between her bodies and through her chakras, no longer caught or compressed. She was lit and radiating from the inside out.

And this process is yours. You will experience this depth within yourself. Maybe not the first time, but through devotion and willingness. Because these parts of yourself want nothing more than to be met by you.

So meet them. Water them. They are literal seeds. What do you do with seeds in the garden? You water them. You water your desires with your attention, with your energy.

Your desires are not destinations. They are invitations. To meet yourself, from the I AM, within the discomfort of the yearning and the process of creation itself.

Meeting Your Desires

Take a moment to breathe into your body. Feel your breath move in and out. Simply feel this. No need to change anything.

Allow yourself to arrive here fully. In this moment, you are not your history, your obligations, or what others have told you is possible. You are simply here.

From here, grant yourself permission to feel and experience your desires. What have you pushed down or dismissed? If failure were impossible and money no obstacle, what would you desire to create? And before the world told you what was possible, what did you want then?

Write it down exactly as you hear it. This is your opportunity to listen fully.

Once you have your desires written down, meet yourself within them. Breathe into the I AM state. Feel your body activate through the phrase. Now, read your desire out loud.

Feel your words in your throat. Observe and witness how your body responds. Breathe here. Nothing needs to be other than what is. Sit here for a few moments.

Now, ask your womb/hara to feel the yearning of the desire. Breathe and allow. There is nothing that has to be accomplished here. Stay in the energy of curiosity. What does it feel like in your body when you invite in the yearning?

What happens in your body? What do you notice? Breathe here. Stay here as long as you can. Repeat the desire out loud to yourself. Allow yourself to meet it in your body. In the yearning, in the ache.

Simply observe here. There is no need to force or attempt to feel anything. Remember, your body is communicating with you. Are you listening? Stay here for a few moments. Then, when you are ready, come back to the room and write down what you experienced.

Remember to hold the energy of the witness here. Can you write what you observed from wholeness? If you notice judgment, don't push it away. Write it down. Meet the judgment. Meet everything that arises here in this moment.

I'm celebrating you for the courage to meet yourself here. I'm celebrating everything that arose in this moment for you. Your desires, your ache, and any separation that showed itself. I invite you to celebrate yourself. This moment of meeting yourself is the entry point into Coherently Creating your desire, your life as Aliveness, worth, and sovereignty.

From that meeting, clarity of action arises like the next scene in a movie. Fluid and expected.

Awareness is your ability to bear witness to the scenes in the movie of your life.

When you focus on your desires, you don't need to try to "figure out" how to create them. And, in fact, this can lead you down the road of performance and force instead of power and creation.

There is nothing for you to figure out.

Focus on them. Love them, and you will begin to receive information on what action to take to create them. More about this in the action chapter.

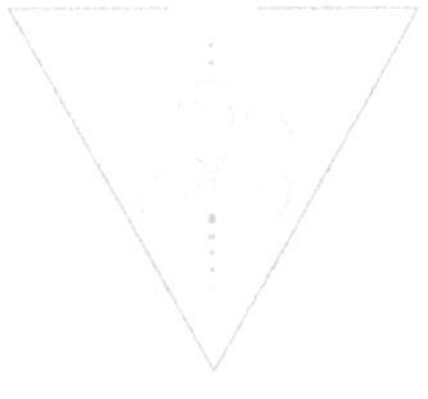

CHAPTER 3

THE LIVING WIRE

During one of my sessions with a client back in 2019, the energy went into her vagus nerve, lighting it up like a network of electrical wires in her body. I didn't actually know what the vagus nerve really was at the time. I simply heard my Higher Self tell me that we were working on it.

At first, I thought nothing of it. But then, in my very next session, the same thing occurred. And in the one after that. This happens often when a particular energy is moving through the collective consciousness. It wasn't the repetition that had me curious. It was the inquiry it had sparked. What is the vagus nerve?

I looked it up and studied it briefly. Then, shortly after, Higher Self told me that humanity needed to slow down. That we could no longer continue the rat race mentality that we had lived for years. Higher Self told me to inform my clients of how to connect to their nervous systems, ground themselves, and be conscious of how much they were putting on their plates.

Then, Higher Self brought through a very clear prophecy. Humans were going to either slow down, or they were going to be forced to slow down. I shared this with my community, even though I didn't honestly know what it meant exactly.

In 2020, the world shut down. Humans were literally forced to slow down. One of the many gifts of that time, whether anyone named it or not, was a collective nervous system reset.

During that time, I was studying the nervous system in more depth and was rather shocked by the pages of generalized and very common symptoms that stem from a dysregulated nervous system. Why was no one talking about this?

I recognized myself in that list. Symptoms I had battled right after my Kundalini awakening, when my body collapsed completely, and no one could tell me why. I had young children who needed everything from me, and I had nothing left to give. I was bound to the couch, exhausted in a way that sleep could not touch. I had always lived an active life: horses, diving, rock climbing, and suddenly I was struggling to simply survive, let alone thrive. I felt broken. Like something had gone deeply wrong, and I had no idea if I would ever find my way back.

None of it felt profound, like the orgasm in the car. This felt like collapse.

I was sent from one specialist to another. Test after test. No diagnosis or answers, just shrugged shoulders and dismissals. At one point, a musculoskeletal specialist ran a machine over my body to trigger my muscles. I told the nurse that it was making me dizzy. She scoffed, disgust written all over her face. "You are being ridiculous," she said.

I immediately fell silent. Like I always had. Like I had been taught to do.

Her face, her reaction, it was familiar. Not this woman specifically, but the moment. Another woman, another scoff, another version of the same verdict. Somehow, I was wrong. Somehow, I was inferior. Not enough. Inadequate. I didn't necessarily believe her. But I didn't reject her either. I submitted. As I always had. Because my nervous system didn't know anything else.

What I declared, I created.
Even in illness. Even in collapse.

The doctors eventually began questioning whether I was making it up, right to my face. I felt crazy. I felt completely alone. I finally stopped looking for answers in conventional medicine and followed a different path.

A functional medicine doctor gave me what years of specialists could not. A diagnosis. Chronic Lyme disease.

I dove into the research. I learned that around the full moon, the spirochetes are most active and that Herxheimer reactions follow. And my body began to fall into that rhythm exactly. Every full moon, right on schedule, the symptoms surged.

Until one day, my Higher Self said, simply and clearly: "Stop."

"Stop telling yourself all of this. Stop identifying with it. From now on, speak from health."

So I did. And that was the turning point. The Lyme disease didn't disappear overnight. But I finally stopped meeting myself as the wound and started to meet myself as wholeness. My body had been responding to my perspective. The more I aligned with the story of separation, the more my nervous system delivered it faithfully. What I declared, I created. Even in illness. Even in collapse. And when I declared wholeness instead, everything began to change.

By the time I found that list of symptoms years later, I no longer had them. I had found my way back to health by meeting myself as the I AM presence and taking action from there. But finding that list didn't bring relief. It brought fury. How different would that entire experience have been if I had seen this list then? The Kundalini awakening had clearly triggered dormant trauma stored in my nervous system. But no one understood that. Not the specialists. Not my doctors. Not even me.

And then I looked at my clients. I saw them on that list, too. Dozens of them. Walking around with symptoms that had names, had roots, had answers, and yet no one had told them either. The knowledge I was reading was not new. It was known. But it was ignored.

It was an awakening.

When the Wire Comes Alive

I started to dive deep into my own nervous system. I found stored trauma and suppressed emotions in layers. Every time I had stifled my voice. Every time I had been bullied as a kid and simply shut down rather than stand up for myself. Every time I had been spanked by my father, a belt in his hand and anger in his eyes. These memories lived in my nervous system, unprocessed. I realized how often I was in a state of freeze or fawn throughout my entire life, thinking that I was simply calm.

That realization was terrifying in its own right. If what I had believed was calm was actually shut down, what was underneath it? It felt like at any moment I could lose control. Of myself. Of my emotions. That I would become like a feral animal whose presence unnerved everyone around it. Unpredictable. Unsafe. What would happen if I allowed myself to unleash this from within? Was numbness and shutdown safer than chaos? Would I always be sensitive and triggered by the smallest of experiences?

These were not small fears. They were the wound of separation speaking through the very process of trying to meet it.

But I kept going.

When I began to work with my nervous system, I was radically awakened to how easily it became stimulated. We were living in Sedona at the time. Most weekends, we would take short trips to the surrounding areas. Every time we left, I could feel us leaving the familiar energy of Sedona, like driving out of a bubble. And on the other side, stimulation. Every hotel arrival, I would have to lie down on the bed and stroke my stomach, following nothing but the instinct of my body. I didn't have many tools yet. I was simply listening.

It initially felt like I had opened a can of worms. Now, instead of shutting down, I felt. And I felt a lot. The smallest things would set off my nervous system. Going somewhere new. Being with my young boys. Moments that seemed completely benign. I began to wonder if I even wanted this sensitivity. How could I actually live feeling everything this acutely? My body, after being ignored my entire life, was screaming at the drop of a hat.

Drama queen.

And I admit, it was annoying. But I knew it mattered. Higher Self had told me it mattered. So I kept listening.

Your nervous system is the mycelium
of your inner world.

After a couple of years of consistent work, not linear, not always willing, but devoted, my nervous system was able to shift in and out of its various states with ease. I could feel each state intimately, and I knew exactly what I needed. And from that knowing, something shifted. My nervous system became a powerful instrument of creation.

I began to drop into flow states I had never accessed before. Deep communion with creation itself. I could feel creation breathing with me, moving with me, as me. Epiphanies arrived viscerally, felt before they were known. The words hummed through my system like the harmony of a violin. Exquisite. Profound clarity that revealed layers upon layers of wisdom, not simply understood, but tasted. Experienced. As if each revelation had its own texture, its own resonance moving through my body.

I move in and out of these flow states, completely immersed in the richness of the moment. Each one an explosion of Aliveness coursing through my nervous system. Not calm. Not quiet. Alive.

The Mycelium Hums

Your nervous system is the mycelium of your inner world. Not metaphorically. It is the living connective tissue that extends your physical body into the subtle realms where the Trinity already exists. It carries intelligence between your organs and, most intimately, between your womb/hara, heart, and Third Eye. It is the network through which the Trinity communicates with you. Through which you communicate with it.

It is the instrument through which you hold the I AM presence while meeting what arises. When the mycelium is frayed with trauma and emotions that were never processed, nothing gets through. You cannot hear your Higher Self. Instead, you hear the voices of the wound. The pain. The not enough. And those voices become the ones running the show. You take action from separation and create more of it. You cannot feel your wholeness because you are not home. You are reacting from trauma that happened years ago, declaring separation without knowing it, and your reality faithfully reflects it back.

I lived this. The nurse. The submission. The full moon cycles my body performed on schedule. All of it was my nervous system running the program it had been given. What I declared, I created.

When Shakti, the creative life force energy, flows through a dysregulated nervous system, it feels like fire moving through your body. Hot wires shocking you from the inside. It creates mental confusion and a lack of discernment. You find yourself repeating patterns and behaviors that you know do not serve you, yet seem to lack the power to break. The energy generally doesn't flow past the solar plexus chakra, causing heightened agitation, stress, and a feeling of always being either triggered or shut down. The energy cannot make it to the heart to expand your capacity for self-love and compassion.

It stays stuck. Stuck in the identity of the past.

There is a specific place in the body where this change occurs. Where the channel between the physical and the subtle opens or closes. Where Shakti either moves freely or remains trapped below.

I noticed this first in those 2019 sessions. When Higher Self directed the energy into the vagus nerve, I could feel the entire physical body and all the subtle bodies responding at once. Like an antenna coming online. Everything in the field shifted simultaneously. I didn't know what it was yet. But I could feel that it was significant. A major component of something I didn't yet have language for.

The vagus nerve holds the physiological key to super-consciousness. To the ability to create in communion with Source. It expresses the essence of the Soul through the physical tissue of the body. Before the Incarnation Blueprint. Before identity and ego. Before the body and physical form. Before mental constructs and human conditioning. Pure.

The tissue of the vagus nerve responds to the creative life force energy that rises as Shakti. It is this tissue that allows Shakti to actualize from potential into form. The vagus nerve harnesses and focuses the wild primordial energy of Shakti, making it usable energy for creation.

It also allows the descent of the Higher Self, of Higher Intelligence, down into the body. This happens to a greater extent after Shakti has risen and met the crown. The feeling is one of being deeply present and available to life through the eyes of your Higher Intelligence. Super-human. Able to access intelligence and channel creative power while surrendering to your Soul's higher knowing. Fluid and vast, yet grounded in the human experience.

In its clearest and most communicative state, the vagus nerve becomes an antenna. A receiver of the energies of the higher bodies. Allowing for deep communion with creation. The direct flow of creation through the body into form.

You become more sensitive to subtle energetic fields. You can feel others more deeply than they feel themselves. You can sense streams of consciousness, known as telepathy. In any given moment, there are dimensional layers of information overlapping each other as waves of energy. You can feel those waves. Sense their qualities, their intelligence, and even their intention. You become a lie detector and a wisdom tuner.

You become a highly tuned instrument of Self.

This is what I actually experience when the mycelium hums. When I drop into the Mother below, her energy rises through the network of my nervous system like nourishment my cells have been waiting for. Not what food gives the body. Something deeper. My meridians light up. My energy flows with a vibrancy the body truly adores. It feels like being fed at the level of the Soul.

The Father descends, like the sun's rays, from the sky. His energy feels like a hand of grace coming down to touch me. Strong yet loving. Supportive yet allowing. My womb responds to him as if she has finally been met. A stability enters my field, and she softens in his embrace.

And the Child. The Child feels eternal. Ancient and wise beyond the human experience. A resonance that reverberates through my entire field. Joyous and playful. I swear I often hear laughter. A giggle. A shriek of delight. My heart lights up, and every chakra responds, opening and expanding to this energy.

When all three merge, I feel like I have everything I need.

That is what a clear nervous system makes possible. The Trinity has always been present, waiting for the channel to open. And this is available to you.

But this does not occur in one fell swoop. It is devotion. The devotion to showing up daily to wherever your nervous system is in that moment. In the agitation. In the numbness. Without a reference point. Without a map. Just you, meeting yourself, again and again and again. Learning to breathe into your nervous system and come home to this moment.

The Trinity Activation

Bring your awareness to your physical body. Take three deep, slow breaths in through your nose, out through your mouth. Cleansing, clearing, and releasing.

Now feel the gentle gravitational pull on your body toward the Earth. Soften here. Allow any tension to be released. Soften your shoulders, face, back, and hips. Soften your muscles. Soften your mind.

Visualize your nervous system. A system of wires within your body. Breathe and connect to this from within. Now visualize this network extending down, through your body, into the Earth. Like mycelium extending down into the soil, into the rock. Breathe.

Here, you connect to Mother as Gaia. Allow yourself to root into her. Allow yourself to connect, feel her. Breathe here. Now allow her energy to enter the mycelium and move up into your body. Into your nervous system. She rises, bringing nourishment into your body. Feel her moving into your cells, your meridians, your energy. Breathe and receive.

Can you feel her energy? What does it feel like moving through your nervous system? Simply observe, no right or wrong here.

Then visualize the mycelium of your body extending upward into the sky, up through the stars to the Grand Central Sun. You know this place. Trust that. Connect here to Father Sun. He descends like rays of light, a hand of grace coming down to meet you. Strong yet loving. Supportive yet allowing. Breathe with him. Receive his light and intelligence down into your body. Into your nervous system.

What does his energy feel like? Does your body soften in his presence? Simply notice.

Now breathe with both: Mother below, Father above. Feel the fluidity, the communication, the love.

Meet yourself here in this moment. Whatever arises is perfect. Breathe into it. Allow it.

Then bring your awareness to your heart and imagine mycelium going into your heart, infinitely. Into Soul. Into Source. A network of mycelium connecting you to everything. To Creation. This is the Child. Ancient. Eternal. Wise beyond the human experience. Breathe here. Feel this connection. Can you feel the resonance moving through your entire field? The joy of it. The playfulness. Receive the energy of Creation through your heart into your nervous system. Breathe and receive.

What does this energy feel like in your heart? Moving through your body?

Now observe all three: below, above, and within. Breathe and allow the energy to circulate. To expand. To flow. Feel the presence of the I AM here. The I AM received through the body, sustained.

No need to control or direct the energy. Allow the intelligence to move at will. Receive and allow.

Take this moment in fully. When ready, open your eyes and bring your awareness back to the room. Notice how you feel without judgment.

This exercise will naturally shift your nervous system through the connection to the Trinity of Creation. The more you practice this, the more connected you will feel to yourself and to the Trinity. Trust that this exercise will evolve with your practice. It will meet you exactly where you are.

And every time you meet yourself in this moment, no matter your state, and you choose wholeness, you awaken Aliveness from within. You choose connection with yourself over disconnection. You will begin to notice the times that you are not fully present to life. You will begin to crave this intimacy of Self.

The theory is a doorway. The mind will always seek more information, but conceptual understanding is not experiential living. It is in the moments you choose this exercise, choose the practices in this book, that you truly grant yourself the power of Coherent Creation.

The Trinity of Creation will deepen your relationship to this network, allowing you to meet life more fully and awaken the Aliveness within.

PART TWO
THE TRINITY OF CREATION

CHAPTER 4

AWARENESS

A client of mine, I'll call her Sarah, struggled to conceive a baby. Sarah desired nothing more, literally nothing else in life, than to be a mother. But she couldn't conceive. It broke her heart.

When she came to me, her shoulders appeared heavy, her entire face fallen. She sighed, melancholy and exhausted, as if even the telling of her story cost her something. She was in a great deal of emotional pain.

The raw edge of having such a clear and strong desire, and the simultaneous feeling of disempowerment to create it, was deflating her. She felt like a balloon that had let out all its air. Part of her wanted to give up entirely.

But the yearning to have a biological child wouldn't go away, no matter how much she tried to ignore it or deny herself the longing. When we began exploring the awareness behind her experience, she was baffled and shocked.

At an early age, she had taken care of her younger sister. And through this, there had been many times her sister experienced something painful that Sarah blamed herself for.

"If only I had done more," she would tell herself.

She took on the suffering of her sister and, when we explored even deeper, her mother. This martyrdom exhausted her. She always felt she had no energy, no spare time, nothing left for herself.

It felt like a gaping hole in the side of a plane mid-flight, where everything is sucked out at high speed. No amount of rest could fill it. No amount of doing more for others could fill it. Because the moment either arrived, it too was swallowed through the hole.

She began to see that she was the emotional water bearer for herself and her entire family. And the moment she saw it, the weight became visceral. Like a heavy backpack she had forgotten she was wearing. Her body adjusted under it, shoulders dropping slightly, as if the recognition itself had added mass. She exhaled through pursed lips, cheeks full, the slow release of someone who had just set down a load they had been carrying for a very long time.

From this place of release, she began to recognize how much she depleted herself for the sake of others. No boundaries. No time or love for herself. This pattern of overgiving and then judging herself for it was the wound she kept returning to.

Her first reaction to seeing that she was a martyr was to condemn herself and feel like she needed to do even more. And this is where the first experience of magic arises.

She met herself in the ever-present wound of not enough. The cycle of judging herself, doing more, still feeling like it wasn't enough, judging herself again. The pattern repeating, relentless. And here, in this moment, we stopped it. We stopped the judgment and brought love through instead.

As I walked her through it, I showed her and allowed her to feel the deeper truth. She connected to a felt knowing that this wasn't a way to live. It wasn't loving to herself. You cannot pour from an empty cup.

Through our process together, she opened up and released the identity that said she had to save others. And from the bind of separation releasing, a spark of insight, of Aliveness, revealed itself. The answer.

The wound was love, turned against itself
by the belief of not enough.

Finally, the answer to why she felt so betrayed by her desires, by her body. The answer she had pursued through the medical system for years. Why? Why can't I conceive? And in that moment, the answer was granted. As truth tremoring from within her cells.

She wasn't a mother yet because she deeply feared the pain of not being a good enough mother to that child. The very depth of her desire was the source of her blockage. The wound was love, turned against itself by the belief of not enough.

She wept. Her body let go of years of why in those tears. Something shuddered through her, soft and deep, like a truth releasing itself from a place that logic had never been able to reach. She was releasing the lie and activating the truth at the same time.

This is how our conscious and subconscious misalign with each other to create the wound of separation. We believe and deeply feel that we desire something, but our subconscious mind holds a belief we cannot yet see

Now, Sarah is choosing herself. She is learning how to create time and space for the things that nourish her, that bring her joy. She still supports her family, but from a place of genuine love rather than compulsion. Her boundaries are clear. Her connection to them, deeper than ever.

As I write this, her father is on his deathbed. And life, in its precise and unsparing way, has given her the exact mirror she needed most.

The pattern that had kept her from motherhood was playing out in its rawest form. The pull to abandon herself. To pour from an empty cup into the ones she loved. To give until there was nothing left of her.

But this time, she could see it. She was able to observe herself from a place of acceptance rather than judgment. She didn't feel not enough. She could see how much value she brought to the moment. She knew, in her body, that she was doing it differently because she chose to meet herself in the moment.

Her Soul had always known. It would not bring a child into a life of self-sacrifice. The desire to be a mother and the pattern of self-abandonment could not coexist. Her desire was pointing her back to the belief of separation from within.

She met that belief as wholeness. And from wholeness, anything is possible.

Your Reality Is Talking

Sarah's transformation began with a single thing. Awareness. The first pillar of Coherent Creation.

Awareness is the expression of the Child within the Trinity of Creation.

The Child is the Spirit, the neutral witness. Unlike the mind, which analyzes and interprets, or the body, which feels and responds, the Child simply experiences from acceptance and innocence.

It is the one who watches without judgment, without agenda, without needing anything to be different. Like a toddler taking in the world with pure curiosity, not labeling it good or bad, simply being present to it. In Coherent Creation, we return to the Child through the eye of the observer.

The mind will change. The body will change. And the observer will witness that change from a state of pure acceptance.

The Child is not the I AM. The I AM exists beyond form, before it. It is not part of the Trinity. It creates the Trinity. Existence, consciousness, and bliss. The ground from which all of Creation arises.

The Child is the neutral principle within form. It holds the pure frequency of love, innocence, and, most importantly, acceptance. The active acceptance of yourself. You cannot meet what you are not willing to accept. And the Child accepts completely. This is what makes awareness the first pillar of Coherent Creation. The quality of acceptance that the observer brings. From that acceptance, separation is met, and wholeness is revealed.

Aliveness awakens through the ability to observe oneself in acceptance. Separation reveals itself in the moments we are pulled into story, through judgment, blame, criticism, where the acceptance of the Child is refused. That is the invitation. Return to the Child. To the innocence. To the wonder.

Without it, you are moving through life looking down at your feet. Like someone who spends an entire trail run staring at the ground in front of them, never once lifting their eyes to the forest around them. The beauty is there. The information is there, but without awareness, you cannot see it.

Your physical reality is what I call the House of Mirrors. Like the maze you find at a county fair, it reflects slightly different distortions of your image back to you. When you can see your reality this way, it becomes a source of information.

Deeper into awareness is self-awareness, the ability to be introspective without judgment. And yet, when we first become self-aware, our natural tendency to judge takes over.

For instance, I had a client who had an attachment to wine. For many years, she hadn't been willing to look at it directly.

When she finally became aware of it, it hit her like a bat to the chest. The word alcoholic circled her head like buzzards preparing to descend on the dead. She immediately pushed the idea away and defended her attachment with, "I just like to drink it while I make dinner."

And there it was. The shame spiral. The awareness arriving, the judgment following instantly behind it, and the defense rising to protect her from both.

But beneath the defense was something more tender. As we stayed with it, what revealed itself was not a woman who lacked willpower or discipline. She was deeply sensitive. Tapped into the energies around her in ways she had never been taught to understand or hold. The world came in loud and fast and full. And the wine turned the volume down.

She wasn't filling a void. She was dampening an overflow. Her own Aliveness, her own sensitivity, had become something she needed to escape from rather than inhabit.

That is what awareness made visible. Not just the attachment. What the attachment was protecting her from. And that is the Golden Nugget hiding inside every shadow we are afraid to look at directly.

This is a common pattern that we all experience on some level. The attachments and shadow actions that we subconsciously convince ourselves are fine, yet deeper within, we harbor shame toward ourselves for those choices.

The first time you truly see the deeper subconscious beliefs creating your actions and patterns, it can be a hard pill to swallow. Much like Neo in *The Matrix*, who had to face the full truth of reality. The truth that reality looked nothing like the lie that was told to him. The lies we tell ourselves about the reality we are creating require this exposure. This honesty.

But shame and judgment will not serve you here. Nothing you ever see or feel defines you unless you allow it to.

All our beliefs and emotions stem from our identity. And that identity is not the fullness of who you are.

It serves only partially in this incarnation. You are an eternal being. Your identity is much more like a role in a movie than the actor itself.   It reminds me of a time when I moved to Honduras to teach scuba diving. My two bags, my entire livelihood, were stolen in transit and never arrived. Everything I owned, everything I had traveled with for years, was gone.

A wonderful woman at one of the dive shops gave me some of her clothes. I was deeply grateful. But I noticed something the moment I put them on. They were not clothes I would personally choose to wear. I felt like a completely different person.

Like the clothes didn't fit right, even though they were the perfect size.

This is your identity in relation to your wholeness. From the outside, it fits perfectly. The world sees it, accepts it, and recognizes it. But from the level of your Soul, it will never feel complete. And that is the point.

Because in the friction of that discomfort, the lessons of life become available. You are here to learn, as a Soul, in a human body. And those lessons arrive through the imperfect expression of identity.

You are not your identity. You are not your thoughts, beliefs, feelings, or emotions. You are none of it. And simultaneously, when you allow yourself to meet these expressions fully, you meet yourself. The Self.

Aliveness occurs when we are willing to face the reflection with love and self-compassion. In that moment of witnessing ourselves, wholeness is remembered, and Aliveness is felt. The colors become more vibrant, and a sense of communion with life is present in the body.

That is the beauty of this work. You exist not in spite of your beliefs and emotions, but as the singer of the song of Creation itself. The one who gives it a voice. Who amplifies its beauty through the harmonics of your body.

When you are able to witness yourself with honesty and transparency, the whole world opens up to you. Awareness leads to what I call the Golden Nugget of any moment, experience, or lesson. The precise wisdom that could not have been thought or analyzed into existence. It arrives through awareness alone. Through the willingness to see.

Sarah's Golden Nugget was this: the very love behind her desire was what was blocking it. Her Soul would not bring a child into a life of self-sacrifice. That wisdom was always there. Awareness is what made it visible.

Awareness, like every aspect of the Trinity of Creation, is a journey with no end to its unfolding.

Information lives in your physical, mental, emotional, and subtle bodies. It moves as wavelengths through densities and dimensions. It exists as every atom of everything. Layers upon layers, overlapping, alive, speaking constantly. The sheer magnitude of what is available to be known is staggering. And all of it is accessible to you through the quality of your awareness.

Now, even though I use the word see, awareness has nothing to do with your physical eyes. It is more like reading between the lines.

When you read a book or watch a film, you can be deeply immersed in it. You can feel what the characters are feeling, moving through the story with them. And yet you remain an observer, not a character in the story.

This is how you want to become aware of your life and of yourself. The identities, beliefs, feelings, and emotions are the characters. They are not who you fundamentally are. Even when you feel them deeply.

The Observer

Take a moment to feel and sense your body and the space around you. Notice how it breathes with you. Feel the weight of your body beneath you. Bring all your awareness into your body. No judgment. Only observe. There is no right or wrong experience here.

What do you notice? Name any sensation, thoughts, or observation without judgment. Notice how your body responds to your own observation of it. Does it soften? Does it tense?

Now shift your awareness to your body and the room. Notice how the container moves from your body to the walls of the room. Can you sense where you dissolve into the room, as the room?

Now zoom out. And observe yourself sitting there, experiencing your body and the room. Notice how the view itself changes. How does this perspective differ from the one inside your body?

What do you observe from here?

Now bring your awareness fully back into your body. Simply let go of any vantage point. Breathe and allow the state of I AM presence to exist from within every cell, photon, and atom of your being.

Notice anything different? Again, this is a skill. Practice it. The more attuned you become with the three different phases, the more aware you become of your awareness. Is your awareness zoomed in or out? Or are you anchored beneath all of it, in the I AM?

You can then move fluidly between the states. Because no state is better than the other. They all have a purpose. Knowing when to be zoomed in so that you can focus on a project or a particular experience will grant you the power of presence. Being able to zoom out will grant you the ability to see different perspectives, see the full picture of any given situation, and gain clarity.

When you allow yourself to dissolve into pure awareness, you begin to see at multiple levels simultaneously. The movie playing out in front of you. The production behind it. And the original script beneath it all. This is the depth that the observer, held in acceptance, makes available to you.

From here, we can go deeper. The why behind anything. Why are you creating what you are creating?

Not from a place of judgment, but from a place of honesty, intimacy, and love.

Just like Sarah, this inquiry can reveal the entire structure behind your current reality. The beliefs, the patterns, the wound of separation quietly running the show beneath the surface. When you can see the structure, you can see where it no longer serves you.

And this is where the quality of your gaze matters. Not the sharp eye of judgment, but the soft eye of love. That is what makes this inquiry safe. That is what makes it possible to see yourself clearly without it becoming another wound.

It is through this quality of presence that you begin to embody more of your Higher Self. Not higher as in better, but from the perspective of a bird's-eye view. The observer who can soar high like the eagle and yet see the tiny details of the pebbles on the ground.

But for now, we deepen our practice of the observer into the structure of your life. All that is required is the willingness to see the truth.

Why are you creating what you are creating? What is truly driving your ship?

The House of Mirrors is that inquiry made alive. Your reality is not passive. It is speaking to you constantly, reflecting back the very structure of what you are creating. All you have to do is learn to listen.

The House of Mirrors

Take a moment to inquire.

What in your life keeps showing up? What pattern, what representation, what circumstance seems to keep circling back into your experience?

That is your House of Mirrors speaking.

Now ask, "What wants to be met here?" No rush. No need for answers.

Instead, allow the moment to swirl around like a piece of delicious chocolate in your mouth, revealing itself to you, layer by layer.

The quality of what reveals itself will also reveal its source.

And so, if what reveals itself is the voice of limitation, that too is your answer. Meet it fully with love. It is pointing directly to the structure of what you are creating.

If nothing arises, that too is perfect. There is never a right or wrong way that this act of communion unfolds. The House of Mirrors will answer. Trust your ability to listen and receive.

Observe your reality over the next few days to a week. I like to imagine that I am casting the question out. I ask it out loud, and then I let it go. I remain present to what arises and observe.

The answer can come from anywhere. Social media, a stranger, a song on the radio, an overheard conversation in a coffee shop. Your job is to remain the observer in order to see, hear, and experience the reflection. The answer will come.

As you begin to observe, write down what arises. No judgment and no attempt to understand. Simply record what is there.

Then sit down with what you have written. Read it not just for what happened, but for what lives beneath it. The event is the movie. The pattern behind it is the production. And beneath both, the original belief that has been quietly directing it all. Allow each layer to reveal itself in its own time. There is no rushing this. The story between the words will speak when you are still enough to hear it.

And ask again, what wants to be met here?

As you sit with what arises, you will begin to hear responses. Answers forming. Voices speaking into the inquiry. And this is where discernment becomes essential. Where is the voice originating from?

Not Every Voice Is Truth

Intuition is a neutral energy. It feels like truth resonating. It carries no emotional charge. The mind's answer, however, feels like a construct.

Think of standing in a church when the organ plays. The sound moves through the walls, through the floor, through your chest before your mind has even registered what it is hearing. You don't decide to feel it. It simply is. That is intuition. It resonates through you because it is already true.

The wound speaks differently. It jabs. It presses. It has the quality of something pushing against you rather than moving through you. It carries charge. Urgency. It wants you to react.

Learning to feel the difference between these two in your body is one of the most valuable skills you will ever develop.

Your Higher Self, the Great Mother, the Great Father, or any guides will speak to you in loving, compassionate ways. Through words, through knowingness, or through felt sense.

If you hear negativity, that is your subconscious mind speaking. Your beliefs about yourself made audible. Just like Sarah heard, "You're not doing enough." That was her wound of not enough speaking.

This distinction is important for two reasons. First, it grants you clarity about where the information is coming from. Second, and this is equally powerful, hearing your subconscious mind speak, when witnessed as the observer, is just as valuable as hearing your intuition or Higher Self.

Because now you have exactly what Sarah had. The awareness of the beliefs that are creating your reality. When that voice comes through, and it will, you can thank it. That is all it is doing. It is not true unless you believe it. Period.

Initially, it can feel like an annoyance. You begin to see it for what it is: just a voice. But over time, it becomes your ally, consistently pointing to the beliefs that no longer serve you.

The most important skill is to remain in the observer. You cannot learn who you are as a sovereign being from a place of self-judgment, criticism, or hate. That isn't sovereignty. You have to be willing to see and experience the deepest, darkest shadow of yourself and know that it is there because it holds light.

Each shadow aspect holds a powerful seed of light and consciousness within it. When you can meet the shadow from love, the wound of separation merges back into wholeness. And the Aliveness that was bound within it is released.

But there is a word of caution I want to extend to you.

There is a trap of "healing" that comes from the "not enough" self. It is an aspect of the human collective, not something unique to any individual. It will tell you that you have to heal yourself. You have to change the belief or the energy.

And while transformation is indeed the outcome of this work, the wisdom is in understanding that you actually transcend a belief or identity when you include it. When you fully love and accept it.

I fell into this trap for years. Telling myself that I was healing myself, but the truth was, I was trying to change myself. Have you ever had someone try to change you? It doesn't feel good. It doesn't feel good when you do it to yourself or to anyone else because it comes from the "not enough" wound. It says you have to change to be worthy, sovereign, and alive.

But true transcendence happens when we can see our shadow, even sit with it intimately, and love ourselves because of it. When we can allow the shadow to become our greatest teacher and ally. When this happens, you transcend the shadow itself.

This isn't about changing yourself from a place of "not enough." It's about becoming intimate with all aspects of yourself, light and shadow, so that you can gain the wisdom and understanding that allow you to embody the worth, sovereignty, and Aliveness that you already are.

That is the art of meeting yourself.

And Embodiment is where you learn to live it.

CHAPTER 5

EMBODIMENT

Embodiment ruptured me from the inside out.

It changed how I showed up to the present moment, how I breathed through challenges, and how I commanded my creative life force energy. Cell by cell, it returned me to the woman I always was.

I was always a deeply sexual person. And yet, when I finally experienced sex, I felt disappointed and confused. It was nothing like I had imagined. Sex did not feel good to me. No orgasmic climax or breathtaking finishes. It felt like sandpaper against my most tender skin.

For many years, I simply thought something was wrong with me. The longing for pleasure that only delivered pain was its own kind of wound.

After my Kundalini awakening, my sexual trauma came roaring to the surface.

In the middle of sex with my then-husband, I would feel the need to scream at him, punch him. Pure rage would well up inside me. But what was I going to do? Hit my husband? For what? Loving on me. I knew it wasn't about him. But I didn't know what to do.

In a split second, I chose to protect him. I chose to hide the madness of it from him. I swallowed it. And in doing so, I took myself down with it. Without warning, I would disappear inside myself, into a pitch-black hole.

It felt like sitting at the bottom of a well. Forgotten. Abandoned. With no way to climb out and no voice to call for help. I couldn't move or talk. He would immediately recognize that something was wrong and attempt to communicate with me. But my words remained stifled. The darkness had consumed me.

Slowly, I would return. But returning didn't solve anything. The well was still there. I just found myself standing beside it again instead of inside it.

I sought help with a wonderful sensuality mentor. She told me to surrender to the wisdom of my body and let the pain move through me. Scream. Hit. Whatever I felt the urge to do.

The rage would surge through my body like an electrical current, and I would let out a soul-shattering wail. My fist would rise, ready to strike, and then drop without ever making contact. It zapped me of every last drop of energy and strength.

I would curl into a ball and cry. I felt like a child having a tantrum. Like a wild beast with no control. Mortified and relieved in the same breath.

After only a few of these experiences, the episodes stopped. But I knew, somewhere beneath the relief, that it wasn't finished. The trauma had gone quiet. It hadn't gone.

But life was anything but calm. Everything happening to me felt like a tornado moving through dry plains, picking up everything in its wake. The marriage ended. Not because of the sexual issues, but because something within me couldn't stay small anymore. Despite our marriage looking wonderful on the outside, on the inside, I felt confined and caged.

And so I left.

Years later, I found Danny, an ex-Navy diver with the most beautiful grin and charismatic personality. We were magnetic from the start, our sexual chemistry intense and undeniable. By this time, I had been practicing embodiment daily, so I was far more attuned to myself.

Only months after being intimate together, the black hole returned. Several years had passed, and yet it drew me in, just as deep and as dark as before. I explained to Danny what he needed to know.

His job was to help me feel safe. Period.

He met me fully. No hesitation in his body, no questioning in his mind, despite not truly understanding what I was going through. Whether I was present or swallowed by the darkness, he stayed. It took an incredible trust between us.

I would scream and rage. I breathed deeply into my yoni, flames rising from my pelvis like hell itself had found a way out. It was painful beyond words.

Trauma, karma, lifetimes of emotional energy came roaring out of my body. Lives lived as a sex slave. Lives of chastisement. Lives where I had lost babies.

My presence anchored me to the moment. To safety. To power. It happened many times.

Finally, through my willingness to meet myself in the trauma, and Danny's unwavering presence, it stopped and never returned.

What emerged was sensation. Pleasure. Full-body orgasm. Cervical orgasms that moved through my body like a symphony, wave upon wave of harmonic ripples sending me into interdimensional worlds, immersing both my partner and me in a deep healing trance for hours afterward.

What the trauma had held captive, embodiment released. A significant amount of my Aliveness, returning home.

Embodiment meets you. In your trauma and in your pleasure. It sings your greatest highs and never abandons you in the lows. If you learn to meet it, it will unlock the Aliveness that craves to be liberated from within.

A craving that even a zombie holds.

Have you ever felt that many humans are not truly alive? As if the zombie movies were onto something? Our society has taught us to live in our heads, in our minds. And while the mind is a powerful tool, when we live there, we don't live here. In the moment. In the presence. In the delicious communion with life.

Embodiment moves you from your head down into your body. And from your body, into the moment, into the challenge, into the creative power that has been waiting there all along. Embodiment is the expression of the Feminine within the Trinity of Creation. She is the body. She is the receiver.

Through the Four Keys of Embodiment, you learn how to meet separation from wholeness and awaken the Aliveness bound within the body. It is not a method given to you by someone else. It is the most intimate relationship you will ever have with yourself. And from that intimacy, creation flows.

The body is the answer.
It always has been.

Many seek this information elsewhere. In past-life regressions, in akashic record readings, and in psychic channels. And these are not wrong. But everything, every memory, every wound, every piece of wisdom your Soul has gathered across lifetimes, is held in the body. The body is the most sophisticated receiver you will ever have access to. It reads the field around you, the subtle energies of others, the intelligence of creation itself. When you learn to inhabit it fully, all of that information becomes available to you. Not through an external reader. Through your own felt sense.

The body is the answer. It always has been.

Where You Meet Yourself

These keys did not arrive all at once. They came through years of living, learning, and listening. The day they crystallized in my awareness, my Higher Self smiled. As if to say, you have been learning these all along.

My three greatest teachers were horses, scuba diving, and yoga. Each one gave me something irreplaceable. You will meet them throughout these pages.

When you practice these keys, you regulate your nervous system, release stored trauma and emotion, and connect to the intelligence of your body. Your intuition sharpens. Your power becomes available. And that power actualizes into your reality, because you have finally learned to meet the one who holds it.

These keys are self-teaching. The more you use them, the deeper they take you. Trust that.

Key of Presence

I was a scuba diving instructor when I first understood what presence truly was.

We were on an open-ocean dive, practicing skills at depth. Skills my students had mastered in the pool. But the ocean is not a pool. It is vast and alive, moving with a power that immediately reminds you that you are a guest.

One of my students had been calm and confident in the pool. But the moment we dropped to depth, I felt it. Her nervous system sending signals into mine. This is not a special gift. It is human. We are wired to feel each other. Most people simply haven't learned to listen.

I could see it in her eyes, too. Fear, quiet but present.

I asked her to remove her mask and replace it. This is a standard skill that she had performed perfectly in the pool.

The moment I signaled her, I felt her fear spike. I moved closer and took hold of her BCD—the jacket that holds the tank—quietly preparing to intervene.

She removed her mask and immediately inhaled water up her nose. In the pool, she had practiced exactly how to handle this: pinch the nose, stop the inhalation, find your breath. She knew what to do.

But fear overtook her, and she panicked.

She spat out her regulator and began clawing her way toward the surface. Time slowed to a crawl as I felt my hand tighten around her BCD. I exhaled powerfully, using my breath to drop our weight down, to stop the ascent.

My heart was beating through my chest. My nervous system contracted. And yet my mind stayed sharp. It felt like standing on the edge of a cliff, feeling the wind attempt to blow you over, but your feet refusing to leave the ground. That was presence. Not the absence of fear. The anchor inside it.

I shoved the regulator back into her mouth and purged it. Pinched her nose gently.

She had inhaled a significant amount of water. Her eyes were wide, her whole body rigid with fear. Her breathing was manic and unstable. She was unstable.

She stopped clawing the moment she felt me pinch her nose and realized she was breathing.

I looked into her eyes. Without a mask, without words, without any way to reach her except through my own stillness. Underwater, you cannot speak. You cannot call out or reassure with language. You have only your presence. And so I poured everything I had into one silent transmission.

You are safe.

I held that vibration with everything in me, knowing she could feel it whether she understood it or not. My other students watched wide-eyed from a few feet away. I was grateful for their stillness.

We stayed there, suspended in the deep, until her breathing slowed. Until her eyes softened. Until she came back.

Then I nodded. She understood. She replaced her mask and cleared the water from it.

Voilà. She was safe.

That was one of many times I held presence for another. I didn't yet fully understand what I was doing. I only knew instinctively that it was what was needed.

I am 5'4". As a female scuba instructor, my students would sometimes look at me and size me up. Quietly questioning whether I had what it took to guide them into the vastness of the unknown.

But presence has nothing to do with size or gender. When you are truly in it, people feel it. Their nervous systems respond to yours. They regulate, soften, and return to themselves. I hold that ability with great honor. Because I know what it cost me to develop it.

When you are in presence, your mind becomes what it was always meant to be. A tool. Not the driver, but the executor of a deeper wisdom.

You are not separate, not from your Higher Self, and not from Source. The ego does not change that truth. It only obscures it, the way fog obscures a landscape that was never actually gone.

In presence, the fog lifts. You see yourself clearly, and you see others clearly. You know the universe as love, and that love becomes the harmony that attunes your life. And the mind, in service to that love, becomes the fingers that move across the strings of the heart.

Spiritual Kung Fu

Bruce Lee said, "Our grand business is not to see what lies dimly at a distance, but to do what lies clearly at our hands."

He understood presence. He is, in fact, the inspiration behind one of my personal favorite teachings. Spiritual Kung Fu.

Spiritual Kung Fu is the art of being so fully present that you are simultaneously relaxed and dynamic. Like a lion at rest, completely still, and yet coiled with the capacity to move in an instant.

From this state, you can sense what is coming before it arrives. Not through thinking, but through feeling. Through communion with life itself. You dissolve into your surroundings the way your body dissolved into the room in the Awareness chapter. And from that merging, you begin to listen to the subtle intelligence of the field.

This moment contains all moments. All potentials exist here, overlapping like radio stations broadcasting simultaneously. In Spiritual Kung Fu, you learn to tune in. To feel which frequencies are most probable, shaped by your current state of being and your intentions. And from that feeling, you respond with precision.

Think of a Kung Fu master. They hardly move. And yet every movement lands with exactly the right force, in exactly the right place, at exactly the right moment. No excess. No waste. Just perfect action arising from perfect presence.

The Kung Fu master. The Jedi Warrior. Different traditions, same truth. Presence is the most powerful energy in any room.

It is the moment after the storm. When the air turns electric, and every sense sharpens at once. It is not just stillness. It is access. When you are truly present, you become available to two distinct layers of information within yourself.

The first is subtle. The etheric. The information that exists beyond the physical, the feelings in a room before anyone has spoken, the knowing that arrives before the mind can explain it, the sense of a probable potential shifting in real time.

Awareness sees. Presence meets.

The second is physical. The body itself. Your triggers, your tension, your gut instinct. The places where old emotions live as stored energy, waiting to be met.

These two layers are not separate. They speak to each other constantly. Presence is what allows you to hear them both. Awareness sees. Presence meets.

They are not the same. Awareness is the observer, the eye that watches without judgment, without agenda. Presence is the embodied meeting. All of you, available. Open. Here.

And that meeting requires relaxation. Not laziness or a lack of doing. But the art of Spiritual Kung Fu. In this state, the current of creative life force energy and therefore information can flow freely through you.

If you imagine clenching your fist as tight as you can and holding it under running water. The water will only be able to penetrate so far because the tension in your fist doesn't allow it to. This is what tension does to creative life force energy: it blocks it.

You Soften Here

Tension is not the enemy. Tension is information. When you feel it, something is asking to be met. But when you tense against the tension—brace against it, numb it, outrun it—you lose access to everything it was trying to show you.

And numbness is more common than we think. You can be wildly successful, deeply functional, admired by everyone around you, and be almost completely numb to your own interior. I know. I was.

Presence is the return. And underneath it, when you soften enough to feel, it is love. Not the emotion. The vibration. The energy of absolute acceptance that underlies everything that exists.

That is what you are returning to. And this homecoming begins with something deceptively simple. Bringing your focus to the here and now.

Where your attention goes, your energy flows. That is the entire teaching in the most cliché and yet truest statement.

Presence is about the quality of your focus. And the body is the most reliable anchor to hold the vessel of focus through the eye of any storm. It is always here, always now.

The mind will wander into the past, into the future, into the noise of everything that isn't. It will follow a thought like a dog follows a scent, completely committed, utterly distracted, and entirely unaware that it has left the room.

Our entire society is built on distraction and has trained your brain to consume rather than to create. And consumption loves the scattered palette of the monkey mind.

So when the mind wanders, and it will, return to the body. Again and again. Without judgment. That returning is where you learn to stop abandoning yourself and meet yourself, no matter what glorious diversion your mind craves.

Presence was one of the most challenging keys for me to teach because initially it seemed vague. "Focus on your body. Be here now." This taught no one anything and led to a great deal of frustration.

How do you practice presence when you have been raised to consume as much content in a single moment as possible? To gorge yourself like a king during a feast. Stuffing your mind full of stimulation, fearing the very silence that you secretly crave.

By focusing on three points at once. I call this the Three Point Focus. This works because it grants the mind permission to not be single-focused, a feat of great measure initially. It works with your mind instead of against it. It gives the mind the task of holding three anchor points at once.

And through that holding, presence becomes possible. This is not about achieving "no mind." That comes later, naturally, as the practice deepens. For now, we begin here. With three points. With the body. With returning.

The three points ARE the Trinity. Touch is the body—the Feminine, grounded, receiving. Sight is the Masculine—focused, projecting, directing. Sound is the Child—the field, the changeless, the ambient intelligence that surrounds everything.

Three points as the Trinity. The infinite fractal of Creation. Aliveness lives here, where these three merge. Always.

The Three Point Focus

Start by bringing your awareness to a point of physical touch. This can be your body touching the seat, your hands folded together, or any other touch point that feels nourishing and supportive.

I like the sit bones because they drop your awareness into your pelvis, grounding you in the moment. However, some people enjoy wrapping their arms around themselves in a warm hug.

Hold your focus on the point of touch. Feel the sensation of it. Zoom your awareness in until only the touch exists. Allow it to consume you. Observe, feel, and meet yourself there. Allow all the tension in your body to melt into it and into the moment.

Let everything else fall away. Stay there for several seconds.

Now bring your awareness to a single point with your eyes. Choose something in your environment that draws you. A spot on the wall, a flicker of light, a detail in the room. Let your gaze soften and settle there.

Hold your focus on that single point. Let your peripheral vision blur and fall away. Allow this one point of light to become your entire world. You are not staring. You are receiving. Let it consume your visual field completely.

Let the world outside this point dissolve while you rest here for several seconds.

Now bring your awareness to sound. Not to identify it or understand it, but simply to receive it. Let the sounds of the room, near and far, wash over you and through you.

Hold your focus on the field of sound. Notice how sound has texture, depth, movement. Allow it to consume you the way water surrounds the body when you sink beneath the surface. You are not listening for anything. You are simply here, in the sound, in the moment.

Let yourself be nowhere else, only here.

Now bring all three together. The point of touch. The point of sight. The field of sound. Hold all three simultaneously. Not with effort, but with the relaxed, dynamic awareness of the lion at rest. If your mind wanders, notice which point you released and return to it. Gently. Without making it mean anything.

This is the convergence of the Trinity within you. As you bring these three points together, notice what you feel. Each point has the potential for its own unique expression of separation. Where you feel nothing, feel tension, or feel the urge to pull away, that is the invitation to meet yourself there and awaken the Aliveness from within.

Practice in stages of thirty seconds at a time, releasing yourself for a few seconds before beginning again. After a few repetitions, begin to extend your stay in the state of presence for slightly longer. Doing this back-to-back enhances your capacity with each repetition.

This is the Three Point Focus. This is presence becoming available to you.

You can also apply this practice directly to your chakras. Place your hand on a chakra as your touch point, bring your gaze and your awareness there, and breathe.

When I was first learning to meditate, this is how I worked. I would move slowly from the root chakra to the crown, holding each one for several minutes. It taught me to feel each center individually, their unique texture, their particular quality of energy.

And through that feeling, I began to meet what lived there.

As the practice deepens, begin to take it into movement. Into simple tasks first, washing dishes, walking, and folding laundry. Notice how presence changes the quality of even the most ordinary moments. Then take it further. Into creative work, into physical exertion, into anything that asks something of you. This is where presence stops being a practice and starts being a way of living.

This is Spiritual Kung Fu in action. And this is where your Higher Self begins to move through you. As a current. Now bring your desire into it.

Take three nice, deep breaths into your body. Allow your awareness to rest on the I AM state. Know it in this moment.

Let it vibrate in every cell, every photon, every atom of your being. Now bring your three focal points in. Breathe. Allow both the focal points and the I AM state to exist simultaneously. Allow the I AM state to inhabit the three points. Feel it. Touch it. Hear it. See it. Create this intimacy with it. Commune here. Stay here for a few breaths.

Now bring in your desire. Notice what arises. Notice if one of the points loses its hold. Or two. Or all three. Bring your awareness back to all three. Notice what you feel in your body. Breathe. Sink deeper into this present moment. Be the I AM and meet your desire at all three points. Feel it. Touch it. Hear it. See it. Be it. Be the desire. Be the yearning of the desire. Be the I AM. All of it existing here and now. Meet yourself here. Stay here as long as you can. Observe what arises. What sensations? What visuals? When ready, come out of the practice and write down what you experienced.

This is where Desire, Awareness, and Embodiment converge. Meet yourself fully in this moment as wholeness, and Aliveness will awaken.

Key of Breath

Yoga taught me breath. Not just the surface-level, and honestly quite boring "inhale and exhale" that you hear ringing in most yoga studios in the West. It taught me how my breath directly affected my body and the energy flowing through it.

A dear friend taught me yoga when I was living in Costa Rica. At the time, I had no interest in meditation or yoga, but when I saw her on her deck, moving with grace between the asanas, I was mesmerized.

She explained the breath to me in great detail and then took me through the series of asanas. Afterward, she lent me a book that allowed me to practice on my own. This was where the practice came alive for me. In those moments, in the heat and humidity of Costa Rica,

I began to connect to the rhythm, power, and fluidity of my breath.

I realized that when I breathed fully and completely, my body would respond and move with the breath. I would breathe in, just as she taught me, and find that my breath extended my spine. I would breathe out and sink into an asana as if it were embracing me there.

My body felt like a snake responding to music. It felt sensual and welcoming. It was as if an ancient door was opening, and the secrets of the universe were revealed. All through the gateway of my breath. And it changed how I carried myself. How I moved. I found myself walking more upright. I found myself breathing into my body differently as I jogged.

Breath wasn't something I just practiced during yoga. It became instrumental in every aspect of my life.

Through my self-practice, my breath became something people noticed. When I attended classes in other parts of the world, instructors would stop to comment on it. Later, when I lived in Maui, I had a dear friend I practiced with regularly. He was moved by the quality of my breath and would tell me so often.

One day, he invited a teacher from Oahu to work with me on the next level of Ashtanga. The man arrived and immediately began moving me through the asanas at speed. I didn't follow. I took my time. I allowed my breath to carry me through each movement the way it always had.

He didn't understand it, and he didn't appreciate it. To him, it was about moving quickly.

My friend tried to draw his attention to my breath. He never looked, never brought himself into the present moment enough to notice. The most powerful lesson that day had nothing to do with the asanas. It was that rushing doesn't suit my body or my mind. A truth I am still learning to this day.

Breath took the presence I had learned in scuba diving and deepened it into my cells. It became the instrument through which I could play my body, my creativity, and my life.

Breath Is Alive

Without breath, we do not exist here on the physical plane. Breath is life. And breath is living intelligence. It connects and merges us, grounds and elevates us, calms and activates us.

It holds all three expressions of the Trinity and laughs at us with its delicious paradoxical nature. It is an incredible tool that deserves full recognition. A tool that, when utilized, bridges the vastness of your infinite self with the finite structure of your human life.

And it is the most powerful instrument for awakening your Aliveness.

It is yours. Always. And yet, somewhere along the way, we forgot how to breathe properly.

When we are born, we naturally breathe rhythmically into our belly and chest. However, as our nervous system becomes increasingly dysregulated, we learn to breathe shallowly over time.

This has a massive effect on our bodies, our immune system, our endocrine system, our digestive system, and our mental and emotional state.

But how often do you hear anyone speaking about the correct way to breathe? And yet it is the most available tool you will ever have. It exists whether you focus on it or not. It can be used at any moment, in any activity, and can create both instant and sustainable results.

There are many modalities of breathwork—circular breathing, box breathing, holotropic breath—and I have explored the majority of them. My personal preference is simplicity. Deep, conscious, complete breathing. It brings us back to our natural state. And with this alone, you don't actually need any other type of breath.

Rather than sitting down for a dedicated breathwork session, you will find greater results in bringing your body back to its natural breath throughout the day. It returns you. On every level.

I often take random deep breaths with audible sighs. When I was first retraining my body, Danny would hear me and ask if I was okay. Now we laugh because I do it all the time. It is interesting to me that an audible sigh, which is a natural mechanism of the body to release stress, is so rare that we often think something is wrong with someone when they do it.

But it feels incredible. My body craves it. And when I need further assistance to move energy, open my body, or drop deeper into presence, I use circular breath in its various forms.

Deep, rhythmic breathing all day, every day. That is the true magic of breathwork.

The foundation of that practice is what I call the Complete Breath.

The Complete Breath activates three stages of the breath simultaneously. In doing so, it stimulates the vagus nerve, the digestive system, the immune system, and the endocrine system.

It naturally brings the physical, emotional, and mental bodies into homeostasis. The more you practice it and make it your new normal, the more accessible it becomes, even through the most challenging moments. It becomes your anchor. Your connection to your true self, your intuition, and your ability to remain fully present no matter the storm.

There is a difference between breathing fully and breathing completely. A full breath fills the lungs. A Complete Breath activates the entire body. That is what we are learning here.

How are you breathing right now?

Simply observe.

I first became aware of the Complete Breath, or my lack thereof, within my body when my Higher Self told me to breathe very strongly into my belly. I tried and found that my stomach hardly moved at all. The abdomen should move out as you inhale and drop in as you exhale. Mine did move, but it did not move well and felt uncomfortable.

I stayed there, focused on my breath for about forty-five minutes. During that time, I was releasing energy, yawning, and moving through various thought patterns. After about forty-five minutes, my belly was quite loose. The next day, when I woke up, I noticed that my skin had broken out at my solar plexus. This was my body releasing the tension I had been holding.

Ever since that day, I have been very aware of any tension I hold there and the tension that others hold.

That tension lives in the first stage of the Complete Breath, which is commonly called belly breathing. It is created with a relaxed abdomen, which can be difficult for many. When our nervous system is dysregulated, the solar plexus region can be rigid and taut.

The second stage lives in the ribs. With inhalation, the lower ribs expand on all sides. With exhalation, they naturally contract.

The third stage lives in the chest. With inhalation, the chest moves out and slightly up. With exhalation, it drops naturally back down.

Together, these three stages are the Complete Breath.

The Complete Breath

Bring your awareness to your body. Notice your breath. Observe it for a moment. Now, through the nose, inhale slowly and deeply down into your belly. Feel your belly move out as you inhale. What does it feel like? Is it flexible, rigid, smooth, tense? Focus here for several breaths.

Now, on your next breath, breathe in through the nose slowly into your belly and allow your breath to naturally move up, causing your ribs to expand. Continue this two-part sequence for a few more breaths.

Finally, breathe deeply and slowly down into your belly, allowing the ribs to expand and the breath to finish at the chest. The chest expands outwards and slightly up. Allow all three parts to happen naturally. They are not completely one after the other, but instead flow.

Imagine your breath as a balloon gently expanding within you. Where it fills freely, you are open. Where it meets resistance, something is waiting. The resistance is where your body holds the belief of separation. This is the opportunity to be present to it as wholeness. Feel it. And meet yourself there. That is where Aliveness awakens.

Stay here. Let the breath find its own rhythm. This is the Complete Breath.

How did your abdomen feel?

The more you practice the Complete Breath, the more it becomes your new normal. Woven into your day rather than reserved for a designated time, it begins to rewrite the body's default. You are telling yourself, over and over, that this matters.

When you need to move energy more actively, release something deeper, or drop into an altered state, I use circular breathing.

Circular breathing is a continuous breath with no pause between the inhale and exhale. It creates a loop of energy through the body that builds momentum, opens the nervous system, and can move what stillness cannot.

When working in this way, breathe in through the nose and out through the mouth. The exhale through the mouth creates a potent release and loosens the jaw, which corresponds directly to the sacrum and pelvis.

The key to circular breathing is depth. Give priority to the depth of your breath over the speed. Breathe deeply into your body, fully and slowly. Find a rhythm that works for you here, in this moment. Oftentimes, after circular breathing for several minutes, you will feel your body open up. This is when you can add more speed to create a higher flow of energy.

You might feel tingling in your body or even dizziness the first time you breathe like this. It is simply the circulation moving into hypoxic areas. Just like when you sit on your foot, and it falls asleep. The pins and needles feeling is the same idea.

If you experience this, trust your body. You might slow your breathing for a moment to allow the dizziness to pass, but try to stay with the breathing. If you do circular breathing regularly, this will stop happening.

Breathe Your Desire

As you become more familiar with your breath, you can begin to direct it. Focus on any area of your body and breathe into it with intention. The breath will follow your awareness. This is where your breath becomes a living practice rather than an exercise. And it is where you meet your desires.

Bring yourself into a state of circular breathing. Find the rhythm that feels good in this moment. Once there, breathe with the I AM presence. Allow the I AM to circulate as the breath. Breathe as it. Receive it as it. Be as it. Feel your body as your breath and the I AM activate together. Stay here for several breaths. Allow yourself to deepen into the experience of this moment.

Now bring your awareness to your desire. Breathe your desire. Breathe it in, pause with it, exhale it out. Allow all that arises as you do this? Meet it as the I AM presence. Nourish your desire with your breath. Feel the desire activate you. Breathe into that activation. Stay in the circular breath and the I AM presence, no matter what arises.

Notice the inhale, the receiving. Receive your desire from the I AM state. Notice the pause, be with your desire as the I AM state. Notice the exhale, move into life with your desire as the I AM state. The Trinity. The I AM. Your desire. Here now. Stay here for as long as you can. Invite yourself to breathe deeper, fuller, and even a bit faster. Activate. Feel. Awaken yourself here in this moment with your breath.

When ready, take the final inhale and hold your breath at the top. Soften all of your muscles. Sit in the I AM. Feel your desire being held by your body, by the I AM. Then, exhale. I recommend staying here for a few more breaths. When ready, write down what you experienced.

There are no limits to the depth you can take this exercise. Breath is the connector between Self, the I AM, and your desire. Continue to practice and play within the exercise. As you deepen your connection to the keys, your body will begin to guide you where it desires you to breathe and how.

Meet yourself there, and Aliveness will awaken.

Key of Expression

My mother was a beautiful singer. I was not. In fact, I was told from an early age that I was tone-deaf and that I couldn't sing. I believed it.

Later, my then-husband would laugh when I tried to sing to our boys as babies. He meant no harm. But it landed in my heart and stayed there, quietly validating every inadequacy I already held about my voice.

My babies didn't judge my voice. They would look up at me with their big eyes and smile the minute I started to sing. They made me believe that my voice mattered. But I let the world tell me otherwise and found myself rarely singing to them despite my own personal enjoyment of it.

One time, during a plant ceremony, the spirit of the plant, Grandmother, came in and told me to open my mouth and allow whatever wanted to emerge. Within her embrace, I surrendered.

Then, from the wombs of the ancients, a waterfall of sounds and languages resounded like nectar from my mouth.

It was as if it were someone else's voice. I didn't recognize the languages, and yet I could strangely understand them. My voice peaked and crescendoed. I traversed the musical scales effortlessly, hitting notes I had never reached before.

I was bewildered. The entire ceremony, my mouth hardly ever shut. My lips even became dry and cracked. The shaman conducting the circle knew exactly what was occurring and lovingly held space for my expression.

After the ceremony, the sounds continued to well up in my throat. My Higher Self told me to express them. So I did, each time judging the peculiar tones and believing that most of it sounded absolutely crazy.

My Higher Self then told me to create circles and invite people in. And I did. Despite my deepest fears and every inadequacy I held around my voice, I held circle after circle, drumming, closing my eyes, and allowing the sounds through me.

Sometimes glasses shattered. Other times, pictures fell off the walls. I had a water fountain with brass bowls that would shift into harmony with my voice. It was wild.

Each time, I half expected to open my eyes and see the room empty. Everyone having left because of the crazy lady singing and speaking in tongues.

But that didn't happen.

I was asked to express online, then asked to express more. I courageously showed up every time. But it wasn't without a flurry of self-doubt and judgment. For the most part, I couldn't even listen to recordings of myself. The sound of them felt like fingers down a chalkboard to the inadequacy within.

It took years. My throat chakra cleared over and over again. I felt fear to the point of intense trembling. I wanted not to open my mouth every single time I was asked to do so. I wanted it to stop. I wanted anything other than what I was being asked to do.

But I kept doing it.

Even after years of building conviction and love for my voice, I found myself one day at a spring at the top of Mt. Shasta. I was with my partner. We had gone there to enjoy the vortex of the space. When we arrived, a circle of people were ending what appeared to be a ceremony or meditation.

This spot was right at the top of the mountain. The fresh spring water bubbled from deep within the mountain, adding depth to the vast and serene view. It was one of those special spots where everyone tends to whisper, despite it being outside.

We sat down quietly. The group closed their circle but remained at the spring. Something began to rise in me. I could feel the familiar lump in my throat as the energy built, waiting for me to open my mouth.

A few of the others began to play singing bowls. The energy in my body and throat increased. My heart raced. My subconscious mind came in with its familiar voice. "This isn't your space. Who are you to bring your voice here?"

But I knew better. With my heart racing, I slowly opened my mouth and began the transmission.

Others joined me with singing bowls, rattles, and one man even began chanting. Together, we created a melody of harmonics and healing frequencies that filled the mountain air.

Was it for me? Was it for them? It was for all of us. We all received that day. I received being received. Light emanated from my mouth, from my heart, and from my womb. So much energy was coursing through my body.

When the transmission was complete, I told my partner it was time to go. Almost everyone else was lying down in a trance. I, too, was in a trance. As we got up to leave, a few people came up to thank us.

My eyes well up right now as I write this. That moment validated a very challenging journey with my voice. It was spontaneous, unrequested, and with strangers. And they received it. They received me. They received what came through me.

After years of feeling that my voice wasn't enough. Rejected even. There on that mountain, in a serendipitous moment, I was seen for my voice. I was heard for my voice.

This day will never leave my heart. The hard work, the days I cried through my own inadequacy, all of it was a beautiful expression of who I am.

And that is the invitation of Key #3. To let it be fully, unapologetically yours.

Your Voice Is Creation

Expression isn't just vocal. We communicate through our body language, the clothes we choose to wear, and our mannerisms. We tell a story of who we are through our art, our actions, and the choices we make in life.

But our voice is a powerful vibrational tool. One that speaks energy into existence. That commands our individual cells and energetic fields. The words we speak, the tone we choose, and the way we articulate ourselves carry our expression into the world around us.

How you express yourself is how you sing
vibration into life.

Do you sing it clearly or slightly muffled? Is it distorted with niceties, or are you impeccable with your words?

Because every single time you speak, you are creating via sound. Our society has largely taught us to be inauthentic for the sake of politeness. We will lie because we don't want to be rude.

Constantly, our expression is misaligned and in vibrational dissonance. When we create this dissonance of vibration, we create dissonance in our reality. A lie is still a lie. Even a white lie is in dissonance. And reality always reflects the truth of what we are actually singing, not what we wish we were.

Your Soul's song naturally desires to sing through you. But through the lens of separation, we collapse into people-pleasing, politeness, and political correctness. Early on, we alter what we say and how we say it to be accepted into society.

This creates an internal disruption, like a crack in the foundation of your Coherent Creation. It is usually so deep and so familiar that you don't even notice it. When I work with clients to awaken their Aliveness, one surprising experience always arises. They organically and ecstatically begin to want to change what they wear.

This happened to me as well. I found myself desiring a completely different wardrobe. And I realized, as I made those choices, that the desire had always been there. I had simply suppressed it. Told myself I wouldn't wear those clothes. Told myself I would only wear nice clothes on special occasions.

That ended when my Aliveness awakened. My nicest clothes are worn every day. No matter what I'm doing.

Because they are the expression of my Aliveness. They want to sing the colors, textures, and styles that my Soul resonates with.

Expression isn't just about clothes. It is about how we speak about ourselves, our lives, and others. Gossip, for instance, is the wound of separation through words. It is not wholeness, carries no Aliveness, and only fuels the ego.

Speaking about another person with love, honor, and reverence will literally light you up inside. Because you are speaking from wholeness. And wholeness always resonates as truth.

It is about every single word that comes out of your mouth, holding the vibration of wholeness. Your words resonate with the truth that exists in your cells. You activate and align yourself. You turn yourself on.

I do this constantly when I transmit for clients. I will send them a voicemail, and as I am speaking it into existence, creative life force energy is surging through my body.

Imagine speaking that way always.

The voice box is where creative energy is actualized into expression. It projects the vibration of creation into the world. And it is not separate from the body's other creative center, the womb/hara.

In utero, the thyroid gland and the tissues that become the reproductive organs develop in overlapping embryological stages before migrating to their final positions in the body. The voice and the womb share the same origin. They remain intimately connected throughout life, which is why trauma held in the Sacral Center often silences the voice, and why opening the voice can unlock creative and sexual energy simultaneously.

Your voice is not just communication. It is your magnetic nature made audible. It is your creative spirit coming alive through song.

Aliveness awakens here when we fully face any expression that is out of integrity and inauthentic. Whether it is the clothes you are wearing, the words you speak, or how you carry yourself. The wound of separation exposes itself here when you dampen, alter, or dismiss your authentic voice.

When you awaken your Aliveness, your voice changes. It deepens, it sharpens, and it becomes more precise. You are likely to find that you have less to say, but what you do say carries the weight and resonance of truth. What is unexpected is how it changes your expression during sex.

After I started allowing myself to tone and speak in tongues, I also started to express a primal feline energy during sex. It is hard for me to even describe the noises that come out of my mouth. Depending on where the energy is in my body, they are sometimes deep-throated and other times high-pitched. There is a purr that seems to vibrationally soften the moment when needed and a roar that cascades the energy from my yoni all the way to my crown.

I make a lot of noise. So much that one time we received a letter from our neighbor in our mailbox saying, "Could you please close your window?" This was in Evergreen, Colorado, where the houses are not close together. Danny and I both laughed. But the letter was clearly written by a woman in soft, rounded letters, and I could literally feel her desire for such an experience in the energy of her handwritten note.

Your expression releases the primordial Feminine within. Yours will look and sound different from mine. And if you are a man, it will be this powerful and magnetic feminine energy expressed through the Masculine. Not soft, but sovereign. The voice that, when it speaks, the room knows exactly where it stands.

Make no mistake, the awakening of your Aliveness within your expression will ripple into every aspect of your life like a sonic boom. Unstoppable. Inevitable.

And it begins with the most intimate sound in your world. Your own voice.

I Am Here. I Love You.

Your voice resonates uniquely with you. It is designed as a tuning fork for your own vibrational field. When you speak to yourself, every single cell, photon, and atom listens. You are both the conductor and the instrument.

There is a reason that three OMs in my own voice cracked me open that morning in the car. Your voice carries your unique vibrational signature. No external sound, no bowl, no binaural beat, no other voice, is tuned to your field the way your own is. You are the most potent instrument available to you.

This matters not only in what you say about yourself, but in how you speak to yourself, from Self, from wholeness.

My favorite way to meet myself with my voice is the statement, "I am here. I love you." No matter what arises, say this to yourself and watch how you soften into your very own being. As always, you are saying the statement from wholeness to the part of you that is in separation.

Bring your awareness to your body right now. Take a few slow, deep breaths and, from presence, observe what sensations are in your body.

When you feel something. Anything. A tingle, warmth, contraction, or even numbness—speak to that feeling and that part of your body. "I am here. I love you." Observe what happens. If nothing, perfect. If everything, perfect. No expectations.

Aliveness awakens, through movement,
when we meet tension
In the softening, it is released

As you do this with yourself, you will communicate with yourself more clearly. Just as in the House of Mirrors exercise, except this is from self to Self. As within, so without. The experience mirrors the same experience with the external reality.

If something arises, a feeling or memory, you can take the practice deeper by saying, "I hear you or I see you or I feel you. I am here. I love you."

The more you do this, the more the interrelationship with the Self is strengthened. This will not only allow you to meet yourself and awaken Aliveness, but it will strengthen your self-trust, your intuition, and your overall self-coherence.

As Aliveness awakens, your capacity to command your field is required. My favorite quote of all time is from Spider-Man: "With great power comes great responsibility." Aliveness is power. It is pure creative life force energy pulsing through your body.

Decree Declare Command

Not responsibility in a formal context, but responsibility as the wisdom of the heart. This practice is what I call Decree, Declare, Command. I have tried to pick just one of those words, but there is something perfect yet again about the Trinity creating the phrase.

Decreeing, Declaring, and Commanding are different from affirming. The difference is that you are not affirming anything. You are orchestrating the creative energy from within into a harmonic symphony.

You can have fun with this by visualizing yourself as a captain on a vessel, a conductor of the finest orchestra, or any image that lights you up.

You have already met the I AM state. Now speak from it.

Breathe into your body. Activate the I AM state from within. Allow yourself a moment to simply connect to that. Feel that. Be that. Now, speak it out loud. Speak it from the full depth of your body, not your throat alone. Make one clear, powerful statement. "I AM." And breathe. Feel what arises in your body. Take another deep breath into your body. Say I AM again, this time feel the vibration through you. As you. Breathe. Observe. Meet everything that is here now.

Say it again, and this time feel your voice, your decree, declare, command, activating your cells, photons, and atoms from within. "I AM". Breathe here. Allow your body to activate. Allow everything to occur.

You may feel resistance as you do this. The parts of you rooted in separation will protest. This practice requires you to be the director of your own inner power. Not controlling, but sovereign. The decree doesn't need the wound's permission. It needs you anchored in wholeness, speaking truth as a decree, declaration, or command. This is Coherent Creation.

You can also use "You are," speaking as the I AM to the parts of you that are ready to be met there fully. "You are safe. You are seen."

Through this deep, intimate connection with yourself, your voice becomes the love that these parts have been waiting for. The love that reminds them of who they truly are. Whole, sovereign, and alive.

Sound Your Desire

When you are ready to take this practice deeper, we can bring in your desire. Breathe down into your body. Feel the presence of your body. Say "I AM" out loud and allow yourself to be activated here. Breathe.

Now, bring your awareness to your desire. Breathe as you hold your awareness on it. Say, "I AM" as you decree, declare, and command that you already are that. That you are the I AM expression of the desire fulfilled. Breathe. Give spaciousness to this moment. Let the power of your voice reverberate into your body, into the space, into your life.

Now invite the opportunity for your desire to express. Does it want to hum, tone, scream, or laugh? What does your desire sound like from the I AM state? Breathe into your body; allow the sound to come. If nothing arises, hum first to initiate sound. Let your desire express.

Fully breathe into your body, remain in the I AM state. Your desire will express itself. Breathe and allow. Give it time. Give it your presence and love. Allow. Keep breathing and allowing. When you are complete, come out of the exercise and write down your experience.

You are now orchestrating the symphony of your cells, awakening your Aliveness from within.

Key of Movement

I was late to bloom socially. When I entered middle school, I felt like everyone around me sped past. I was a tomboy who didn't have a taste for fashion, social cliques, or fitting in.

In a time of my life when I felt very alone, my horse gave me what humans couldn't or wouldn't. Connection. Partnership. And ultimately, communion with creation via the bond between us.

Riding felt like a dance. We waltzed around the arena together, as one. Just like dancers at a ball, inseparable. Joined at the hips, responding to each other's bodies.

I felt as if my horse understood me when no one else did. Understood me without words. Without the need to explain myself. She could feel me, all of me, even the parts that I couldn't feel myself.

When you are connected to your horse, the communication is telepathic and empathic. The rider and horse feel each other, understand what the other is thinking and needing. They become one.

Which, as the rider, is exhilarating. The horse's body is incredibly powerful and athletic, and when you are truly connected, that power moves through you both.

One day, my trainer was yelling at me because I was holding my right side rigid. The minute she started to yell, my body didn't feel safe. Its natural instinct was to tense even more.

As I went around the arena, my left knee slammed into the wall, hitting the knobs that protruded from it, causing me intense pain. I tried to relax. But my trainer kept yelling. The more I tensed, the more my horse tensed, and the worse it became. Then my trainer would yell more and trigger the entire cycle again.

I was crying in pain. Crying because I couldn't get my body to listen to me.

That day, I walked away in tears. Feeling broken.

The next day, by myself, I went to my mare before I even mounted. I spoke to her. I told her that we were okay. I told her it wasn't her fault. She pushed her head into my chest. I cried, feeling heard and courageous. I wasn't going to be broken.

In the saddle, I could feel my body return to the day before. The memory immediately triggered tension. I felt my mare tense, her ears turning back toward me for guidance. In that moment, I said, "You are safe." I was speaking to her. I was speaking to myself.

I felt my body relax. I focused on every muscle being both relaxed and engaged. I softened into my mare's back. She softened into me. We were safe.

Brilliant dance partners are anything but tense. With trust, they flow like breath itself, in and out, without effort, without end.

Aliveness awakens through movement when we meet tension. In the softening, it is released.

Where Energy Becomes Form

Movement is where Shakti meets the physical. It is the first act of creation, moving from within the body outward into the world. And it is why the action that follows embodiment is fundamentally different from the action that follows thought.

Movement is the balance to stillness. Both are needed. Stillness connects you to the thread of creation that never changes: isness, beingness, existence. Movement brings that energy into actualization.

In the context of the Four Keys of Embodiment, movement is in the feminine form. There is no outcome to reach, no destination to arrive at. Only the free flow of pure allowance.

Flowing in the feminine form is listening to how the body desires to move. Not following a script, not directing an outcome. Simply allowing.

When we surrender to our creative life force energy, it moves of its own accord. The pressure dissolves. The need to figure it out dissolves. What remains is the body, moving as it knows how.

This is a practice of letting go and listening. We release our desire to control the movement and hold instead what I call engaged surrender. The body is fully present, fully available, following the intelligence of what wants to move through it.

Life is like dancing. And in all honesty, we are not the leader. The leader is our Higher Self. We are the follower. And the follower must listen carefully to the cues given by the leader.

I often have clients tell me that they don't have clarity or that they don't know the answer. And yet, as soon as we simply take their awareness to the body and ask the question, the answer arrives. It is rare that we don't have an intuitive hit or answer. It is usually the case that we don't want to listen to it, or we choose not to listen out of fear.

And that fear has a root. From the wound of separation, we believe that we are not enough. That our bodies are not enough. How could they possibly hold wisdom? How could they instinctively know what to do? And so we control our bodies for fear of how we look. What others will think. We perform.

Because surrendering to the body feels like trusting something we have been taught not to trust.

But the body knows. It has always known. The follower in the dance is not passive. They are exquisitely present, reading every subtle signal, responding from a place of deep listening. It requires an incredible depth of courage.

But that courage arises from the remembrance of wholeness and meets the wound of separation head-on. Here, Aliveness awakens.

That is the invitation of Key #4.

The more you allow the free flow of movement in your body, the more you will desire to allow the free flow of movement in your life. Because there is no separation between the two. As within, so without.

This is the bridge into action. When you learn to move from within, from the body, from Shakti, from the intelligence of creative life force energy, the actions you take in the world carry that same quality. They arise from presence rather than performance. From listening rather than forcing. From the follower in the dance rather than the ego insisting on the lead.

This is the action that coherently creates from wholeness.

The ocean taught me this as a scuba diver. The ocean is even more powerful than a horse. The difference is that the ocean does not desire to move with me, and instead, it insists that I learn how to move with it. Or struggle. There really is no middle ground.

I learned to listen very carefully to the ocean. Not with my ears, but with my entire being. Listening with my intuition. You have to feel Her, the ocean. You have to allow the water in your body to resonate with the water all around you, as if you are dissolving into her vastness and yet working from your sovereignty.

Fighting her power is simply silly. And it will exhaust you. Instead, you learn how to move your body in a way that flows with her currents, with her surge.

Have you ever sat in shallow water and felt the ebb and flow of the waves? That feeling when you simply float and let go of trying to be anywhere specifically? That is the feeling. That is what we are practicing here.

Engaged Surrender

Can you listen and move with the flow of your creative life force energy? Can you surrender and be in a centered readiness for the next move?

Movement begins most easily from movement already in motion. Much like a pendulum, it moves far more freely from inertia than from stillness.

Begin with something simple. Rocking, swaying, moving in slow circles. Let the body find its rhythm before you ask anything of it. From there, you can begin to listen and transition into engaged surrender.

Be fully present with your body and allow it to show you where it craves movement. Is it in your hips? As you breathe into them and rock them back and forth, do they ask for something erratic? Something asymmetrical?

Sometimes the body will find a movement and ask you to sink into a repetition there. This can support the release of tension within the soft tissue. Notice where you feel tension. Ask the body what it would like there to support the softening.

Walking can also serve this process, but only when there is no destination. I love walking around the island in my kitchen for exactly this reason. No trail, no direction, no arrival point. Just the body moving for the joy of moving.

All of this—the rocking, the kitchen island—invites the same thing. Your body moving freely, without an agenda. And your mind will have opinions about that. What arises? Does it judge? These thoughts are completely normal. Remember to observe from wholeness and bring your awareness fully back to your body.

Do you feel any tension as those thoughts come in? Where in your body do you feel that tension? Ask your body how to meet the tension. What movement will meet the tension? With presence and breath, listen to your body like the ocean's waves and surges. Let your body move you, and there, the Aliveness awakens.

And sometimes, the most powerful way to meet the tension is through play.

If your mind is judging the movement as ridiculous, for a moment, over-emphasize the ridiculousness. Take yourself from full, free movement and allow yourself to express "silly" and "ridiculous" in the most playful way possible. It can shift the judgment of oneself faster than anything else.

One time, my body was working through some energy, and I found myself lifting bent legs up high with my chest up and shoulders back. I felt like a chicken. I laughed at this thought and simply played into it. I allowed the chicken energy to be explored playfully while my body was enjoying the movement.

My body didn't stay there long, and I shifted into a different expression. There was never any judgment of the chicken dance. Only play and exploration. We are primal beings, and animal energies can come through quite often. Maybe it is with the feet and legs, maybe it is with the hands and arms. Either way, you are working with the consciousness and genius of that animal.

Have fun with it. Laugh at yourself from a place of love and joy. Children have no idea that there are "ways to dance." They simply move how they want, and they are filled with joy in the process.

This is the freedom your body already knows.

Move Your Desire

Take some nice, deep breaths into your body.

Connect here with your body. You might hug yourself, run your hands over your body, or begin with simple movements. Breathe. Bring in the I AM state. Feel the resonance of that state in your body. Visualize, feel every cell light up as the I AM. Breathe.

Now bring in your desire. Meet your desire as the I AM. Feel that in your body. Now ask your desire, how it wants to move. What type of movement does your desire feel like? What type of movement feels like it moves your desire through your body? Hold the I AM state, breathe, and allow.

Be connected to your body here. Be connected to your desire here. No need for it to look like anything. No need for anything to happen. Give permission. Flow with it as it shifts and changes within you. Breathe. Do this until your body says it's complete.

If you were standing, sit down. Feel your body after you come back into stillness. Be in the I AM state. What do you notice? What do you feel? When ready, write down your answers.

This way of moving awakens the Aliveness within and connects you deeply to the current of creation. From its flow, action simply is.

Combining the Keys

The keys work wonders by themselves. And, like instruments, when we combine them, they move from a single source into a symphony of sound.

The process of combination is deeply intuitive. The more you practice each key by itself, the stronger a relationship you will have with that key and thus the communication of how that key wishes to combine with the others.

There is no formula. Mastery is always rooted in your own body. You are the master of your reality, and therefore, you hold the wisdom of how to unlock and activate it.

There is no limit to the levels of mastery. Mastery is not a destination. Mastery is a journey to the higher levels of consciousness expressed in human form. And the keys can take you on that journey. They will naturally guide you into higher expressions of your own brilliance and lead you down the path of life that is most alive.

You may find yourself using all four simultaneously or weaving between them. There is no right or wrong. Presence and breath are always the foundation. From there, your body will know what it needs and when it needs it. Your only responsibility is to listen.

As presence deepens, stillness becomes the ground beneath all movement. You begin to zoom in and out of experience itself, from the tiniest sensation to the full canvas of your life, with the fluid ease of an eagle in flight. Breath moves through all of it, because breath always is. It exists whether you direct it or not. And when breath meets presence, something profound occurs. The paradox of change and changelessness. God felt in the body.

From that ground, expression rises. The Shakti moves up and out of the mouth as healing tones, as primal sound, as the power to command your own energies. Pleasure becomes a portal. Sensuality becomes communion. And when movement joins, when the body is present, breathing, and expressing simultaneously, something ancient awakens. Sexual magic. Creative fire moving through every layer of your being at once.

When all four merge, time slows. You begin to feel the potential you are creating before they actualize. You sense which ones are yours and which ones are not. You choose. That is Spiritual Kung Fu.

Primal Intelligence

And the most primal of instruments is already within you.

Your cells, photons, and atoms love even the most basic of sounds. Just like a baby that is soothed by its mother humming a melody.

Humming is one of the most underrated tools available to you. When you hum, you will feel your nervous system hum in tandem with the sound of your voice.

Like a vibration moving through your body, activating and stabilizing yourself. It also activates the vocal cords gently, warming the voice before deeper expression. And because it requires no words, no structure, and no performance, it meets you exactly where you are.

Toning—sustaining a single vowel sound or pitch—takes this further. It creates resonance in the body, clearing stagnant energy and opening the channels through which your creative life force moves. Different tones resonate with different centers of the body. You will feel this instinctively as you explore.

There is no wrong way to hum or tone. Simply begin. Follow what your body wants to sound. This is your voice learning to trust itself before it speaks.

As any great musician knows, the ability to riff is the art of communion with creation itself. To be fully present to what is naturally flowing through the sound of your voice and body, moving with that channel rather than directing it.

I call this Circuitry Reprogramming. It is not only powerful; it is fun.

Circuitry Reprogramming

The entire point is to release structure. To be present in the moment and the authentic expression that desires to resonate through your being. Just like when Grandmother told me to simply open my mouth and let it flow.

When you do this, you connect to the wisdom of love within you. You will channel phrases, expressions, and words that are dynamic for that moment. It will activate you like nothing else.

To do this, I recommend warming up your voice first. You can use the Decree, Declare, Command exercise for this, or you can simply hum and tone the sound that feels intuitively aligned. Resonate.

Do this for a minute. Then, breathe into your body, open your mouth, and allow the words to flow. Speak as love. Speak as wisdom.

The delight here is in the natural dynamism of the moment. You might find that what flows repeats itself for several days or even weeks. And then, without warning, it shifts into something else entirely. This is consciousness moving through you. Trust it. Trust yourself.

This is the beginning taste of what it feels like to Ecstatically Create.

It is experiencing the creative life force in its Aliveness as it courses through your body. Like an elixir, the fountain of youth. It is enhancing this elixir per the needs of your body. It is bringing this elixir through the unique fractal that is your genius to ignite your surroundings with Aliveness.

It is going inward to the depths of self that you have not yet journeyed. Exploding outward with epiphany and wisdom. All four combined are pure magic that has no bottom, top, or sides to the infinite potential that you can experience yourself as Source.

This is embodiment. Not a technique. Not a practice you do and then put down. It is the living, breathing, moment-to-moment experience of being fully alive in your human form. When you embody all Four Keys together, you stop performing your life and start creating it. You stop managing your reality and start dancing with it. The Four Keys of Embodiment are not the destination. They are how you learn to walk the path with your whole self. And that changes everything.

CHAPTER 6

ACTION

My client, I'll call her Meredith, had money issues. No matter how much she made, it disappeared. More income brought more bills. More success brought more drama. The excess was always stripped away, as if some invisible hand refused to let it stay.

One time, her car broke down and required thousands of dollars in repairs. Another time, a family member became very ill, and she had to spend thousands of dollars to visit them in the hospital and take time off work. The bills always appeared to be out of her control. They seemingly dropped in out of nowhere.

She was in a constant state of worry. She didn't feel safe with money and didn't understand why. She felt powerless. It seemed unfair to her. As if others were given a golden spoon, and she had to eat with a stick. It made her angry, envious, and spiteful.

She found herself unable to feel grateful, even though she saw her life as beautiful. She knew that we are all inherently abundant, but her life was not reflecting that. She felt like a failure.

She would say things like, "Money doesn't grow on trees," and "I never have enough money." When she came to me, she felt defeated by life. She knew that she didn't want to live like this anymore, but she didn't know how to change it.

Meredith, honestly, didn't have much hope left. Like she was showing up for a movie, already guessing what the ending would look like. She had been there, done that, when it came to "manifesting abundance." But it was like her wallet wouldn't listen.

When we began to explore her relationship with money, a clear pattern emerged. As already mentioned, money would disappear as quickly as it came. But we also noticed her tension and contraction every single time she had to spend it.

Meredith told me that it felt like a vise around her gut. Squeezing tightly. So tight that she oftentimes felt like she couldn't breathe.

When we dug deeper, we found limiting beliefs about money that came from her family. She had grown up in a rather poor household. Her mother didn't work, so every penny came from her father. There was always a conversation about something being too expensive or not being able to afford something else.

Her parents also had regular fights about money. Her father would blow up and yell at her mother for spending money that he felt they didn't have, while her mother felt like she was buying necessities for the family. It was a tension that hung in the air like bad cologne.

She had breathed that tension in for years. And without knowing it, she had carried it with her into every financial decision she had ever made.

The most profound realization we had was around the quality of her actions. Her state of being when she worked with money. She was always checking her bank account from a place of fear. Spending from fear. Earning from fear. Every single action was rooted in fear.

She would go on shopping sprees and spend money on things she didn't truly want, only to feel shame afterward. Meredith said that the shame was so intense that she often took most of it back and drowned her sorrows in a pint of ice cream.

The fear didn't only show up in how she spent. It showed up in how she received. She undercharged in her chiropractic business and often gave enormous discounts or free sessions. These weren't acts of kindness. They were acts of lack.

Action can look like one thing but hold the energy of another. We often think we are being generous or kind when, in fact, we are taking action from limitation, from the identity of not enough. This is what Meredith was doing.

All of her actions around money said one thing: "I don't trust it."

She didn't trust that she could earn it or keep it. She didn't trust herself to have it. She didn't trust money itself and subconsciously believed it was evil.

There were many more layers than this. But the point is clear. Although she was "managing her money" on the outside, every action she took came from the energy of not enough.

After Meredith met herself in her own lack, she began to notice the energy she was in when she checked her bank account, asked a client to pay, or felt the urge to spend on things she didn't need. Each time she was able to observe, she had a choice: change the quality of the action, change the energy, or repeat the same pattern with the same energy.

Sometimes, she was aware that she was choosing to repeat the process even though she no longer desired it.

Then came the shame. And this is the beautiful unraveling. The shame was painful. Part of her wanted to dissociate, go shopping, not look at her bank account, and distract herself. But she met herself in the shame. She learned how to love herself there. She learned that the shame was not who she was. It was simply pointing to a belief that she held about herself.

She stopped the shame loop, and she began to take action from a different why. Why? Because she was sovereign and worthy. Why? Because she was choosing to see money from this truth.

The shift was not overnight, but it was not slow either. She started to feel a sense of ease with money. She created clearer boundaries around pricing in her business. She raised her prices, and her clients happily paid. Her shopping sprees became intentional and joyous rather than compulsive and shameful.

But the biggest shift was that she started to recognize her own value. Not just as a business owner, but as a woman, as a friend, as a human being. That recognition translated into every aspect of her life. Money stopped being the enemy. It became an ally.

One day, she said to me, "I feel like money has my back."

And it did. Because she finally had her own.

It doesn't have to take years. It can happen immediately when you meet separation as wholeness and awaken the Aliveness within.

Just as the fertilization of an egg happens in the blink of an eye, once the preparation and clarity are complete.

Arrow of Action

Without action, creative life force energy arises as potential but then dissolves back down. It is the egg that is not fertilized and, therefore, shed every cycle. The Feminine creative energy requires the Masculine for creation. He is the sperm that activates the intelligence of the egg. He is the spark of light that initiates potential into form. He is the structure that gives potential direction.

As I mentioned, action actualizes energy into form. It is the inner Masculine of the Trinity of Creation. You can think of it like a bow and arrow. Each time you take an action, you are shooting an arrow into the quantum field, informing it what you are creating.

The Masculine's role is to actualize creative life force energy from wholeness. We do this by listening to our inner wisdom. By not taking action simply to fill the void in our schedules. The moment the Masculine is doing in order to get, he is disconnected from wholeness. And therefore, you are working from a place of separation.

I call this performance. And it is rampant in humanity solely because we have not been taught these deeper spiritual truths. Even in spirituality, much has come down to ego mechanisms of manifestation rather than creating from unity.

Performance is the Masculine expressing the belief of separation. It creates a co-dependency between doing and receiving. The Masculine does in order to get, and the Feminine receives with expectation. It is duality expressing itself through the mechanisms of action and reception.

This is Fragmented Creation. Coherent Creation is the free flow of creative life force energy through you into form. If you are doing in order to get, or receiving with expectation or obligation, you are in the belief of separation.

Doing in order to get feels like a child waiting for candy after finishing their chores. The truth is, you wouldn't be doing the chores if there weren't candy waiting at the finish line. All you can think about is that candy. And when the reward comes, it lacks. Because the mind creates an expectation that reality rarely matches.

This is experienced on the receiving side, too. If you receive a favor from a friend, you feel you have to return it. If you are an entrepreneur charging a high price, you feel you have to deliver in some calculated, equal measure. In a career, the higher the rank, the heavier the weight of expectation to perform and deliver.

Neither is free. Neither is whole.

When you meet yourself in the separation that says you have to do anything in order to get, you awaken Aliveness through the process of choice. You can chase the carrot dangling in front of your face, or you can take the action that feels integral and sovereign, regardless of the result.

And with receiving, it is the same. You can choose to receive simply because you exist. Receive from the choice of wholeness, from an open heart. Receive fully and deeply, with honor and respect. That way of receiving is far superior to receiving with obligation. The quality of the action of receiving is rooted in sovereignty and worth.

Power arises from wholeness. It is self-sustaining because it is aligned with the intelligence of creation itself.

Performance doesn't honor creation. It thinks in quantity. In quotas. In metrics. Because separation is always trying to prove enough-ness. The Masculine in performance will overdrive, overwork, and overdo. But when you take action from wholeness, you have nothing to prove. Quantity naturally drops. Quality naturally rises. Each action holds more power and more potency. Spiritual Kung Fu.

Humanity has placed a great deal of emphasis on action while lacking in awareness altogether. The grind and hustle culture of our society is a symptom of this. Force requires continuous momentum to maintain its creation. The moment it stops, the creation collapses. It is exhausting by nature.

Power arises from wholeness. It is self-sustaining because it is aligned with the intelligence of creation itself. It doesn't need to be maintained. It grows. Because power serves the whole, it fuels itself. Like thousands of tiny streams leading into a river, and eventually the ocean. Only to evaporate and return to the streams. Self-sourced.

In the human experience, that is sovereign action.

When Danny and I moved back to Colorado, he found a job before our arrival that would pay him $15k to relocate. It was perfect. However, after we arrived, he found that he didn't align with the company. They had poor integrity, choosing to cut corners rather than make choices that benefited the whole. They placed considerable weight on him as a safety manager while simultaneously undermining his decisions. They said they desired safety, but their actions showed otherwise.

In his contract, it stated that if he left before a year of employment, he would have to pay back the $15k. He couldn't do that.

He felt the weight of the $15k looming over him, as if it wanted to hold him hostage to a lie. His chest felt tight as his mind turned in circles of litigation and the headache that followed. His logical self told him to take the responsible route and stay until he could pay back the money.

But he recognized that feeling in his gut. The one that told him that to stay meant self-abandonment. It meant agreeing to the belief of separation. Like an ex-lover who texts you out of the blue, trying to rekindle what was. He wasn't having it.

He turned to me. I reminded him that he couldn't make decisions out of fear. He immediately agreed. And as fear met truth within him, he felt a surge of inspiration. He wasn't going to allow anyone or anything to define who he was. He applied for positions with a list of local companies, standing tall in the conviction that integrity mattered.

Within a week, the company dissolved his position along with seven other employees. In the dissolution letter, they wrote that he owed them nothing. Shortly after, he found a new position with a company that shared his values entirely.

Danny was elated. It was the perfect solution to a problem that hadn't appeared to have one. In a moment that often feels like stress, the job dissolving instead felt like Divine Orchestration. It felt like the universe was on his side. We celebrated.

Because he chose to take action from sovereignty rather than lack, the field responded.

Action is a choice. The choice to meet separation as wholeness, and then to back that choice through movement in the world.

Quality of Action

We all know the statement: actions speak louder than words. And it is true. But not just any action fits that bill. It is the action that validates the truth. The truth that you are whole. The truth that your desires are in service of that wholeness. And action is the mechanism through which you articulate it.

This is what Danny did. Not perfectly, not without fear. But when fear arose, he met it with wholeness. And he moved from that place. That is Coherent Creation through action.

And in that moment of choosing sovereignty over separation, Aliveness awakens.

Meredith experienced this same truth through every action she took around money. Not all action is created equally. An action can seem like one thing but hold a completely different truth through the lens of awareness. Like Meredith, you can be giving from a place of lack instead of a place of true kindness and self-love. The quality of those actions is radically different, and each arrow informs the field in a completely different way.

Creation doesn't respond to what the action is. It responds to the intention of the action itself.

The arrow of lack tells the field that separation is your truth. The arrow of self-love and kindness tells the field that wholeness is your truth. Creation always responds to what you believe yourself to be, not to what you are trying to get. And from the House of Mirrors, what you embody is what is reflected.

This is why so many people give endlessly and feel resentful that nothing returns. They are giving from the identity of not enough—doing in order to get—while telling themselves it is kindness. The ego is very good at that particular disguise.

When they recognize the identity of not enough and meet it with love, they meet separation as wholeness. And there, Aliveness awakens.

Learn how to take quality action, and your reality shifts.

Quality action begins with you listening deeply to your own wisdom, to your wholeness. It requires you to recognize the deeper why behind your actions and to devote yourself to clarity of what you are truly creating.

You first ask yourself why. Why do you want what you desire? The trick here is not to take the first answer that comes to mind. Usually, that comes from the ego, which is eager to fill in the blanks. It will give you something that sounds true but sits on the surface. You are going deeper than that.

Instead, it is most powerful to ask a series of whys.

Follow the Thread

So start with a desire, and ask yourself, "Why do I desire to create this?" Write down the answer. Now ask, from that answer, "Why do I desire that?" Write down the answer. Keep doing this for at least four rounds. Go until there are no other answers to why. And then switch to "therefore."

From your last answer to "why," ask "and therefore" and fill in the blank. "Therefore" is a sideways movement. Where "why" takes you deeper, "therefore" sidesteps the conscious mind to allow another perspective and more depth.

From that answer, start again with why. Keep doing this until you hit it. You will know when you do. It is like a tuning fork going off in your body. You will feel it.

Let me give you an example from a session with a client. She wanted to create $100k a month in her business.

"Why do you want that?" Her answer: "Because then I can create anything I want."

"Why do you want to create anything you want?" Her answer: "Because then I will feel free."

This is where she stopped. She landed on freedom and said, "Yep, that's it." And truthfully, it was a part of her Core Desire. But I felt called to take it further.

"And therefore?" Her answer: "And therefore, not be controlled by anyone or anything."

Now, it is important to note here that using negative words will create more challenges in the exercise. So "not be controlled" needs to flip to the other side of that coin. When I invited her to do that, she said, "Be in my personal power."

"Why do you want to be in your personal power?" Her answer: "Because it feels good to me. It feels true."

"And therefore?" Her answer: "And therefore, I believe in myself."

When the words came out of her mouth, her mouth stayed agape, and her eyes were wide. I could feel her drop immediately into her body. Into her wholeness. She started crying. It was never about the money or the success. It was about believing in herself. And as we explored a bit further, trusting herself.

It was as if she finally saw and met that truth in the moment of desire. Her energetic field was open and available to her own genius. From there, I taught her how to take action from self-belief and self-trust. And everything changed.

After that day, her next offer roared in. It was something she had never thought about before. She launched it and almost immediately sold three. She couldn't believe it. She even checked the transactions herself because her mind was challenging it.

But it wasn't about the sales. For her, it was the deeper truth of what she desired and the clarity of that moment. From that clarity, she was able to take action that served her wholeness, her genius.

Taking action from your Core Desire is the action that will actually create it. This doesn't mean that you spend all of your money because you are "taking action from abundance." If you do the why exercise, you will find that the actual why has nothing to do with spending money.

If your action is causing you more suffering or stress, you haven't yet found your Core Desire.

And if you don't know what you actually desire, you can't create it. This is why so many people create lives of wealth, success, and status and find themselves miserable. Their ego convinced them that was what they truly wanted. But it was only a shadow of their Core Desire. And from that shadow, their reality reflected the same.

Find your Core Desire and take action from there.

Action Ignited

Bring your awareness to your Core Desire. Breathe into the I AM state. Feel the I AM activate you at a cellular level. Breathe deeply into your body. Feel the yearning of your desire in your body and meet yourself there. Does it desire you to express? Or move? How can you meet it in this moment fully?

Be fully present and available. Use the Four Keys to deepen your communion with it now.

What arises? Do you feel worthy, sovereign, and alive? Or do you feel separate, lacking, and disconnected? There is no right or wrong here. Be in a full state of observation and presence with yourself. Feel it. Be with it, as it. There is no rush here. Allow nothing or everything to occur. Stay with this until you feel like your body is complete.

Then, if you are standing, sit down. Breathe into your body and rest in the I AM state. Ask for direction. "What action is aligned now?"

Listen and breathe. No expectation that anything arises. Just be with the stillness. Notice how the mind will tell you that you need to act now. But oftentimes, the action will arise later. This isn't about getting an answer. It's about meeting yourself and inviting the question.

When you are complete, write down what you experienced.

Spaciousness—a teaching that deepens in Ecstatic Creation—is granting presence to the moment without anything needing to happen. It is the art of being so fully here that creation has room to blossom. To reveal its next petal of beauty to you. It is profound and, in my experience, always results in clarity.

This moment, when you feel separation and choose not to take action from that place, is the choice of the arrow. It is where you determine the quality of action that you cast into the field. It is the moment of reconciliation with yourself. Give it the space it needs. Use the Four Keys to meet yourself, to awaken the Aliveness that is awaiting you here in this moment.

When you feel that you are in wholeness, the action will become very clear to you. It will feel neutral, like the perfect temperature. Aligned. An obvious choice. It will feel inspirational yet grounded.

From here, you no longer delay. You take action. Because intuitive hits have windows of time connected to them. Each moment has layers of information and alignments. If you wait, you risk taking the right action at the wrong time.

The windows of time are dynamic and specific to each action. Don't overthink what I am saying. Take action as soon as you know it. The rest will follow as the flow of creation from within.

I had a reading with an astrologer about my business one day. As he was going through my chart, he paused. "You have love coming in," he told me, "very clearly." I wasn't looking for love and felt a bit annoyed. He said, "Like it or not, it's coming."

Sure enough, a few months later, my Higher Self told me to go on dating apps. I had never been on a dating app and truly had no desire whatsoever. I honestly didn't want to waste my time. But I listened.

The minute I opened the app, I saw Danny. I felt the resonance, that pull immediately. The kind you feel toward someone the moment you see them. Something in me knew. But I had convinced myself that I needed a spiritual man. So I talked myself out of it and went on a few very failed dates with said spiritual men.

Which only increased the frustration I already held toward this idea of love when I wasn't looking. See, I'm wasting my time, I thought to myself. But my Higher Self told me to get back on the app. I was hesitant and resistant. Like a teenager being asked to clean their room. I'm sure I even did the eye roll. But the minute I opened it, Danny was there again.

This time, I leaned in. I reached out, and he immediately responded. I remember the first time we spoke on the phone, his voice activated me. I felt like a schoolgirl.

We started dating on February 2, 2020. Only a few months later, the entire world shut down.

Our chemistry and connection were obvious from the start. So while everyone went into lockdown, we went into full hook-up mode. We spent every moment together. Movies, ordering out, waiting in the car while they brought us our food with masks on. We became inseparable.

We were both so grateful to have each other during that time. If I had missed that window, lockdown would have been a very different experience. I had several friends who experienced it by themselves. They felt lonely and cut off from the world. But Danny and I had each other.

If I had ignored my Higher Self, I would have missed the window. Would I have been given another chance? Maybe. Maybe not.

Missing the moment holds a higher cost than meeting the resistance. Any resistance to taking action is simply a point of separation. When you meet that moment, Aliveness awakens.

And once you do, once you take that action from wholeness, your only remaining task is to release it completely.

After the Arrow Flies

The minute the arrow leaves the bow, the trajectory is set. The quality of action has been actualized and needs no more of your attention. You don't need to keep opening the oven to check on the food. Every time you do, you let out the heat. You slow the creation. And in fact, when we do that, we become attached to the outcome.

Attachment kills creation.

Creation is non-linear and doesn't always reveal its full inner workings to the physical eye. You can't always see what is cooking. The mind desires to know. But attachment isn't action from wholeness. It is action from lack.

Do you fully trust what you are creating? Or are you still unsure? The answer will be revealed the minute the arrow is released.

This is where you learn to practice non-attachment. Non-attachment is not detachment or indifference. It is not a state of not caring or not taking responsibility for your actions. It is the state of allowance for what arises from the quality of your actions.

Detachment is refusing to look at the reflection from the House of Mirrors altogether. It is the state of denial that leads to spiritual bypassing.

The best way to practice non-attachment is from the space of curiosity. With an open mind and inquisitiveness. The energy, once again, of the Child. Observing your reality with wonder at what is about to be revealed.

Non-attachment creates opportunities for the big pivots in life. The ones that alter the course of your reality. A leap of faith.

Leaps of faith are not required to create your heart's desires or to blossom into your Creative Genius. But they do tend to create a radical shift in direction and a quicker establishment of new energies and beliefs within your field. They are the biggest arrow you will ever release.

When my Higher Self guided me to leave my marriage, it felt like truth ringing through my body while simultaneously being hit by a tsunami of fear. How would I even? My mind raced between the logistics and the emotional truth that both my husband and I would be hurt. It raced to my boys and the impact on their lives. The logic screamed in my face that I would be an idiot to make that decision. And yet, I knew it was exactly what I had to do.

There was nothing truly wrong with my relationship. My husband was very loving. We had a beautiful home and two young boys. But my Higher Self showed me that my journey forward needed to be deeply inward. I needed to be fully devoted to my own process and that alone.

It felt selfish. And that word had followed me my entire life. I had learned young that taking action from my own knowing, even when that knowing would ultimately serve everyone, could look, from the outside, like harm. Like abandonment. Like not caring enough about the people I loved.

Many of my family and friends left. They took his side. I was the one breaking up the family. The one who had everything and chose to burn it all down. No one could see what I could feel. That staying would have cost us both more than leaving ever could.

And so I chose the harder right over the easier wrong. Not without grief. Not without the weight of what it cost.

It is never without fear. It is never without doubt. But there is always a wave of potential lifting me toward the direction of the decision. I feel this sense that I can choose not to go down that road, but that the other decisions will actually be more painful. I become aware of the potential that the decision is granting me, and I take the leap.

It's not always perfect. In fact, it's usually messy. But creation is messy. Have you ever noticed how messy a Creator Mother Gaia is? Creations fail all the time under her watch.

Some of the greatest geniuses were known for their messy spaces. Studies have even shown that a messy environment promotes creativity. Messy people often possess "cognitive disinhibition," a trait where the brain filters out fewer "unimportant" stimuli, allowing for unexpected connections and innovative thoughts.

Because the feminine energy of creation is messy and non-linear, she is void. Action Ignited comes from the connection to her.

Notice if you require a perfectly orderly environment. Do you feel uncomfortable the minute something seems out of place? I'm not speaking to a dirty, unhygienic environment. I'm speaking to a disheveled one.

The ability to allow disorder is the exact power of creation. And in Coherent Creation, your most powerful action will come from what appears to be non-linear and illogical action. Can you allow it?

When I enter into a deep current of creation, I often find myself tidying up before it comes. I don't necessarily know it's coming, but my intuition knows. Much like a mother's instinct to nest. I will clean up my space completely. But in the depth of my creative Aliveness, my work area appears very disorganized.

After I move through that particular flow of creative life force energy, I will find myself naturally returning my space to more organization. But I am far from rigidly ordered in this area. I would much prefer to direct my creative energy to the act of creating than to cleaning.

Again, there is no right or wrong here. But if you are naturally very organized, you will find that the idea of Action Ignited might feel very challenging. Most likely, you will need to spend more time in stillness to activate the right hemisphere of your brain so that you can access the full depth of your Creative Genius.

Be willing to meet yourself in the discomfort of messiness.

Because sometimes, the willingness to take messy action. Misaligned action. Not the highest quality of action, but being fully present to the reflection is more powerful than not taking action.

You have to give yourself the power to make mistakes. If you can truly understand this concept and live it, you will grant yourself the great experience of being human.

You will create, sometimes fail, and oftentimes succeed. You will fall flat on your face, but you will learn and grow each and every time. And that, my love, is the entire "point" or "purpose" of being human.

So be messy. But retain your awareness of the mess, the failures, the successes. Because awareness is precisely what beginner's luck lacks. And that is dangerous.

I remember one time I played a new board game and I won, effortlessly, as if I had been playing for years. But the truth is, I had no idea how I succeeded. I couldn't reproduce it. And I especially couldn't reproduce it because the second and even third time around, my mind was attached to perfection.

The stress of that pressure to perform was its own natural-born killer. I was failing before I even started.

It is much more valuable to fail or half succeed, see from a state of awareness what you created, adjust, and create again. This is learning. This is growth.

Meet your messiness from your wholeness. Allow Action Ignited to lead you through the process. Trust that you are worthy and sovereign, and the art of Coherent Creation will move through you with grace.

You have met yourself in the most tender of moments. You have continuously chosen wholeness. Now you move into the Spiral of Aliveness, where you deepen intimately into yourself as the Creative Genius of your reality.

PART THREE
THE SPIRAL OF ALIVENESS

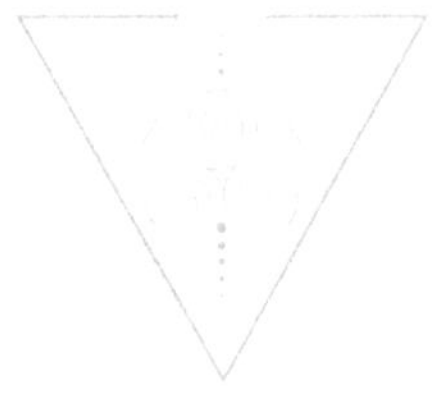

CHAPTER 7

SHAKTI RISE

After my Kundalini awakening, the journey was not over. In fact, it had just begun. Over the years, my Shakti would amplify and expand.

One time, she expanded so intensely that I found myself oscillating between bliss and contraction. A wave of ecstasy would flow through me, and then my entire body would convulse. After many hours of this, I felt like a prisoner in my own body. A passenger with no ability to stop what was moving through me. I held a knowing that it would eventually cease, but desperation had long since replaced that knowing by the time I finally reached out for help.

I tried meditation. I tried grounding. Nothing was stopping it. I reached out to a shaman who had helped me in the past with my Shakti. He understood it better than I did, and in that moment, I felt seen. Met in an experience that very few people in the world could even comprehend.

He told me to drink milk. I didn't consume dairy. He told me to eat meat. I didn't eat meat. Finally, after a pause, he said, "Go put your bare feet on the ground." I walked outside to my backyard. It was a beautiful day, so I stood in the sunlight on the grass.

I remember standing there, barefoot and humbled. Six hours of something vast moving through me, stopped by the earth beneath my feet. I stood in full surrender to Mother Gaia and her power. Almost immediately, the waves stopped.

I went back inside and lay down. In the relief, my mind wandered to the day before. I had experienced a complete dissolution into Source. There was no me. No body, no identity, no separation. Just the vast, boundless presence of what I can only call God.

When I came out of the experience, it took me hours to even want to move. Nothing felt real. My body wasn't real. The room I was in wasn't real. I could feel the waves of energy flowing through us, my body and the room, as a single, uninterrupted expression. I couldn't tell where I ended and the room began.

There was no doer within me. There was no identity or desire. I could have sat there for the rest of my life in absolute completion. But after a couple of hours, my body began to call me back. Much like stepping out of a warm hot tub into the frigid air of a winter night, returning to the room felt jarring. I followed it reluctantly. Some part of me didn't want to return to the physical reality that now struck me as illusory.

But in the middle of the night, I awoke to an ecstatic energy coursing through my body.

I breathed into it. I opened and received it fully. Then all the muscles in my body contracted at once. Tight. I struggled to catch my breath. Then another wave. Then another contraction. It went on like this for hours.

By the time I called the shaman, I was deeply exhausted. My muscles were sore from hours of contracting. I just wanted it to stop.

There were countless other times, usually after an expansive experience, when I would wake up in the middle of the night with what felt like hot electricity pulsing through my body. It was annoyingly painful and relentless. Sleep was not an option. Once again, I felt like I had no control, and all I could do was surrender to the experience.

Every time, I would breathe into it. My Higher Self would inform me that it was my Shakti expanding. She would reach the crown, and I would dissolve once again into oneness. Merged into pure existence. Then she would settle into a particular chakra, and I would be working with that energy for months, sometimes years. Witnessing as the House of Mirrors communicated and reflected the distortions I held there. Taking each moment to meet myself. Aliveness awakening.

This evolution of expanding to the crown and then deepening was at first disorienting. Like adjusting the beam of a flashlight, wide open into the vastness of unification, then narrowed into the focused intensity of a single chakra. But after a few cycles, it became a pattern I could rely on.

Rhythmic in nature.

After many years, the intensity of her expansion stopped feeling like hot electricity and more like warm honey.

I never had any control, nor did I try to. I still, to this day, do nothing to force or even point my Shakti anywhere. Over the years, I have read different exercises to work with Shakti, but every time I went to do them, it felt as if Shakti herself slapped my hand. Without words, she reminded me of her inherent wisdom. Who was I to know better?

Instead, I have found that meeting her in my body, in the moment, has granted me more than any mentally constructed exercise ever could.

Serpent of Wisdom

Shakti is the wisdom of the Divine Feminine. She is responsible for our expansion, our evolutionary journey, and ultimately, our union with the Divine Masculine.

Shakti is an essential part of Creator Consciousness as she is the creative life force energy. Her journey is our personal journey, and her union with her beloved is our union of Self. She both awakens us to the process of unification and meets us in the human experience of creation.

She is the pure potential that inhabits every moment and awakens the Aliveness within.

Shakti is not something you generate. She is not a resource to be cultivated or a power to be earned. She is what was always moving beneath the separation. The obstruction was never her absence. It was the wound of separation. When you meet the wound from wholeness, as the I AM, you are not creating Shakti. You are removing what blocked her flow. She was always there. She has always been there. The meeting is what frees her.

Through the Four Keys of Embodiment, you naturally awaken Shakti. And when awakened, she activates each Creator Center in its unique archetype of creation. Which, in turn, deepens your communion with yourself and your body. A cycle that feeds into itself.

Generally, Shakti is spoken of as the energy of the Goddess that rises from the root to the crown to unite with her beloved, Shiva, in Divine Union. And while this has absolutely been my personal experience, I have been shown and taught by my Higher Self that her wisdom and movement extend far beyond this single description.

I say her because she represents the Divine Feminine within us all. Everyone has Shakti energy, regardless of the body you inhabit or how you identify. And now, on this planet, it is her time to rise once again to meet her beloved. The time for Divine Union within us all.

Union is first and foremost with the Self. Your inner union will create union externally. The pattern of seeking this union outside of ourselves, before we have addressed why we do not already feel unified, is the result of the core wound of separation. That is why Shakti is so vital to this journey. She meets the wound in the innocence of her desire to reunite. She represents the ultimate seeking of self union.

Before Shakti awakens, your relationship with your body narrows. Consider a hose that is kinked. It can only allow so much water to move through it. More pressure is required, but less flow is achieved. That effort is the suffering of humanity. The effort to create. The effort to commune and connect.

When Shakti has not yet awakened, intimacy lives largely in the mind. You may feel it in your body, and that matters. But true intimacy is unification. Because there, nothing can be hidden, denied, or clung to.

And without that intimacy, you cannot hear creation as clearly. You cannot feel what ignites you, where the natural flow of your creative energy desires to move.

Oftentimes, people don't even know what they truly desire when Shakti is dormant. They might name goals or ambitions, but nothing stirs. No yearning from within. It is simply a mental concept. An ego want.

Life in this state has a particular quality. The focus narrows to ego wants projected outward into physical reality. It is about doing in order to get. But it never satiates, never fulfills. This is Fragmented Creation. One thing after another, wondering why the arrival never feels like enough.

The identity runs the show. You become both the one achieving and the one still unfulfilled, identifying with everything you feel and think. Every experience, every emotion, every thought becomes who you are. Holding the point of the observer is much more challenging from this state.

You feel shame toward yourself and your life. The wound of not enough humming in the background, undercutting everything you do and create. So even when you create something that is from Soul, you cannot experience it that way. It feels muted and bland in flavor. It passes as quickly as it climaxed.

This was my personal experience before my Shakti awakened. I have tremendous compassion for it. And if you see yourself in these words, know that these teachings are here for you. They desire to meet you, so that you can meet yourself.

Nothing in these words defines who you are. They point to experiences. Valid experiences at that. All relevant to your journey.

Shakti meets you in that wound. Not as your ego screaming, "You are not enough," but as Aliveness awakening within your being.

How She Moves

Her devotional journey begins at the root with one clear desire, unification with Shiva, who awaits her at the threshold of the crown. This is the quintessential story of Shakti. Shakti does indeed travel up to the crown. However, in my experience, she does not only travel in a linear fashion. It is often felt that way in the body, starting at her seat and rising through the central channel. But when I drop into a more subtle awareness, I feel her moving through dual channels in a spiral.

What's even more fascinating is that she spirals outward as she rises, moving through chakras that exist outside of the physical form entirely. She moves through your entire light body.

Knowing how and where she is moving is not important. As you work with her, you will begin to sense her more fully. However, her movement is always best left to the intelligence of her wisdom, not your mind.

When you meet her in the moment, in your body, you deepen the relationship we have been building throughout this entire journey, to your own energy, your own wisdom, your own Self. This is Coherent Creation. The communion with every aspect of Self from a state of wholeness.

The ego is the only one that seeks a destination. Your heart will always offer you the space you need to move through what arises. And Shakti will activate whatever dormant energies are ready to be met. Trust in the unfolding of this intelligence through your body and life.

My experience was unusually intense. In truth, I have never met another person who has experienced the same level of activation. What unfolds for you will be uniquely yours. Whatever that looks like, however subtle or gradual, is perfect for you and for where you are on your journey.

When we learn to actively work with our Shakti, we learn the movement of our creative life force energy. We learn how it feels to engage ecstatically with our bodies and our lives. We learn that ecstatic energy lives in everything, that even pain can be felt as pleasure. We learn how to use our own inner life force to meet and move through challenges as wholeness.

When she does reach the crown, we experience the unity, bliss, and ecstasy of our natural state. This is our birthright as humans. Just like the experience that Kona showed me of merging back with her Indigo body.

Our Shakti is the inner power that awakens us to it.

She begins as the coiled serpent, awaiting awakening. In this form, she is Kundalini. The potential. Once the awakening begins, she becomes the spirit of Shakti, the movement, the process of returning to oneness. The primordial Feminine on her quest to reunite with the Masculine. Where duality meets itself, and the Child is born anew.

The more you work with your Shakti, the more you will feel her. Initially, you might not feel anything. Whatever you experience is perfect. Continue to use the Four Keys of Embodiment and trust in your own power and ability to open and expand.

Shakti can be felt as a variety of sensations. You might feel pressure or tension. You might feel heat or cold. You might feel numbness or intense emotion. Allow the expression to be authentic. Some days and months might be quiet while others burn with her fire. Feel where she is and meet yourself there.

Like a pilgrimage to a sacred site, you journey with her.

Stoke the Fire

The seat of your Shakti is located just above the root chakra, at the center of your body. This is where she coils, where she waits, where she stirs. Drop your awareness here and breathe. Take three deep cleansing breaths in through your nose and out through your mouth as you come fully into the here and now.

Hold your focus on her seat. What do you feel? Can you feel the serpent energy? Can you feel the potential coiled? You might feel drawn to sway your body or rock your pelvis back and forth.

Take a moment to bring the energy of honor and reverence to the seat. Greet her with love. Breathe into the I AM state. Meet her from there.

Now, imagine that as you breathe, you are stoking the fire of her essence. Breathe deeply and fully. Hold your focus.

Stay here, communing with her for as long as feels intuitively right. You could spend weeks or even months at this point alone. When ready, move into fire breath. It is a rapid, continuous breath through the nose, both inhale and exhale, quick and shallow.

This breath is activating. Hold your awareness on her seat and breathe for at least ten minutes. Be deeply present to your body and her energy. Can you feel her activating? Can you feel her moving? If you feel her moving, maintain your awareness on her seat as much as possible.

Continue to stoke the fire. After ten minutes of fire breath, squeeze your perineum and anus and draw them upward. This will invite movement without force. Hold your breath here, with these muscles clenched, for as long as you can.

When you release, sit in stillness. Can you feel her? What do you feel? Connect with what arises. Observe.

As you progress, you can begin to follow the movement of Shakti and use the Four Keys of Embodiment to meet any energy she settles on. This will be noted by an area of tension or discomfort in the body, or on a more subtle level, within your field.

The advanced practices are to work with your Shakti in your subtle bodies, the transpersonal chakras, and even within the quantum field.

When working with the subtle bodies, you might feel her move into them. Take your awareness there and use the Four Keys of Embodiment to meet whatever arises. You might also be brought an emotion or a belief structure. Use your intention to locate that energy within your subtle bodies and meet it there, fully. Continue to work with yourself here. Trust where you are guided, and the process will naturally unfold.

There is no end to this spiral of evolution in the awakening and rising of your Shakti.

Exposure. Communion. Existence.

In working with Shakti over many years, and through witnessing hundreds of client experiences, I have been shown three distinct phases of Shakti.

The first phase is exposure. Shakti rises, and all that blocks her flow in the physical body is exposed. The emotions, the traumas, the wounds of this life, your ancestral lineage, and past lives. This phase can be intense. Disorienting. There will be flickering moments of bliss and oneness, but they will feel temporary as the deeper layers surface to be met. This is the most vulnerable phase. It asks a great deal of you. It requires devotion and the willingness to move through the fire of creation.

But if you are able to meet yourself in these moments, in the pain, in the disorientation and confusion, you will begin to truly know yourself. You will begin to reconnect to a part of you that you had lost. Aliveness will awaken for the first time. In fleeting glimpses of moments not abandoned but met.

Despite the discomfort, it is a treasure. And though it is confronting, what you are meeting is the wound of separation. Without this meeting, it exists in your subconscious, running the show.

This phase is where you move from Fragmented Creation into Coherent Creation.

The second phase is communion. The densest layers have been met. Shakti begins to flow with less resistance, and something shifts. The ego loosens its grip. There is less existential crisis, less mental noise. In its place, something quieter arrives. Peace. Love. A deepening sense of being held by something vast.

It feels like being a young child with a loving parent nearby. You are free to explore, to play, to wander. And beneath that freedom is the knowledge that you are supported. That something vast and loving has its eyes on you. Not controlling. Not directing. Simply there. Holding you in every moment.

You begin to breathe again. Spaciousness arrives where the fire was. Time slows, and you slow with it. Instead of trying to climb out of a hole, you find yourself enjoying the creation of your life. Taking it in. Tasting it. You begin to see beyond your own patterns and into the larger field of humanity. Compassion arises naturally. You realize you are not in competition with anyone. You are simply a thread in something much larger.

This phase offers something profound. It is the ability to see all as love. All as creation. This is the moment where suffering becomes grace.

The third phase is existence. There is nothing left to achieve. Nothing left to become. The doing falls away. Energy flows continuously. Life becomes simple. You unfold, rest, and learn. Because you have finally stopped chasing, fighting, or doing in order to get. This is where Ecstatic Creation lives. And in this phase, the rapture of creation moves you as the surf moves through the ocean.

These phases are not linear. You will move between them. You will return to the first even as you taste the third. That is the spiral nature of Shakti herself.

The foundation of the spiral is acceptance. Integration only occurs within the energy of acceptance of self. Meeting yourself in a state of wholeness, worth, and sovereignty.

Shakti deepens and awakens the communion with creation through the Three Creator Centers.

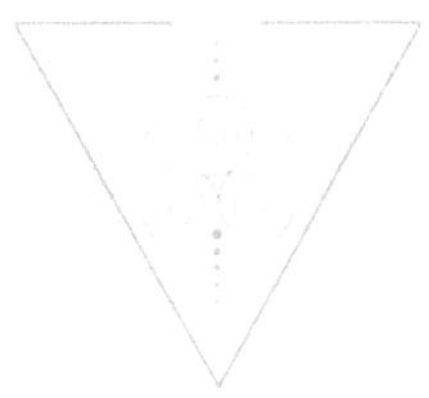

CHAPTER 8

THE THREE CREATOR CENTERS

When Tim came to me, his hair was disheveled, and his beard held the shadow of days of growth. He looked like a man who had stopped taking care of himself. He was a professional writer, but his writing had completely ceased, and he didn't understand why. He had tried all the usual writer's block remedies, but still found himself staring at an empty page.

His overall demeanor felt dampened. His voice was low, and his energy matched it. He was struggling. Struggling to pay the bills because he wasn't writing. Struggling to connect with other people because he was feeling down about himself. He had stopped seeing friends and found himself doing very little with his days.

In his mind, there was no logical reason for the writer's block. He had a clear story in his head, the full arc laid out, the personalities of each character in full color. Yet when he sat down to write, nothing. He would feel a heavy weight on his chest, like the split second before bad news lands in the body. Blank pages stared back at him like a snow-scaped meadow. No story, no creativity, just white.

Writing was his genius, and in these months, he felt far from it. Disconnected. As if he had lost his greatest gift. Only the silence of the stillness filled the air.

In our first session, his body knew exactly why he was blocked. The minute we dropped into his body, he saw an image of his dog, Oliver. He seemed surprised. But with a giant sigh that almost sounded like his own last breath, he shared that Oliver had died about six months ago.

When he shared this, I felt the grief pierce his heart. But beneath it, something heavier. Remorse. As if he believed he hadn't done enough. As if the weight of Oliver's death rested on his shoulders. Oliver, he told me, was his heart dog. That once-in-a-lifetime dog that is like no other.

Oliver had been with him since he was a puppy. They had gone everywhere together. Camping trips, fishing, and even long road trips. But where Tim's voice shifted was the minute he told me how Oliver used to sit right next to him when he wrote, like a companion and perhaps even a muse.

I asked Tim if Oliver had inspired his writing. His voice dropped to almost a whisper, as if speaking the words would invite the pain. "He always made me laugh," he said softly. "I felt so much joy around him." And as the words left his mouth, a memory awakened. His entire face lit up.

Tim told me that Oliver had a way of pulling him out of his writer's block. The minute he felt stuck, he would go play with Oliver and, upon returning, the block was gone. Every single time. Soft tears rolled down his cheeks as the memories played like movies in his head.

Oliver was the one who returned him to joy so effortlessly that Tim had never even recognized it as a creative tool. He had simply lived the moment with his best friend.

Losing Oliver had been the hardest experience of his life. He had pulled back from his friends and family. He didn't desire to connect with anyone else. He just wanted Oliver back.

I couldn't give him Oliver back, but what I could do was help him process his grief. Over a period of time, we worked gently with his heart. He began feeling more joy and gratitude again. But the writing didn't resume.

As we explored deeper, we found something beneath the grief. A fear of connection had settled into his Sacral Center. Tim had lost the most important being in his life and, without realizing it, had decided that connecting that deeply again wasn't worth the risk. But connection, at its deepest, is communion with creation itself.

That same fear was restricting the flow of his creative life force energy. The grief had closed his heart. The fear had shut down his creative fire.

He could feel the truth of it in his body as I spoke. Everything felt emotionally distant, he told me. Like colors seen through frosted glass, still there but dull, unreachable. He had lost his empathy. For a writer whose craft was built on feeling the emotional truth of his characters, that loss cut to the very root of his creative identity.

We worked gently with Tim's Sacral Center to release the distrust and suppression. Within weeks, he found himself absolutely lit up in his writing. It was as if the kink in the hose had been released. The story that had sat in his head came storming through. He told me he didn't sleep much for an entire week. He simply couldn't stop.

But the most interesting part of this experience for Tim was that through his process, he started to feel Oliver's presence. Something he had felt briefly since his passing, but it would always leave. Now it stayed.

Bashfully, Tim told me that he had started talking to Oliver again as if he were right there beside him. He worried it meant he was losing his mind. But what he felt in those moments wasn't madness. It was warmth.

A love that moved through the room and settled in his chest. And through it, something unexpected. The fear of connection began to soften. Oliver had taught him, even in death, that love doesn't only end in loss.

Tim's journey was not just about grief. It was about the inseparable nature of the three centers within him. His story is the teaching made alive. Through my own personal experience, I have learned the power of these three centers and their roles in Coherent Creation.

The Trinity Within You

When I entered into spiritual teachings and meditations, the primary teaching was to work from the heart. And I don't disagree with this. However, the heart is only one of the Three Creator Centers. The Sacral Center is hardly mentioned, and the Third Eye is treated as a psychic novelty rather than a Creator Center.

But my own wisdom taught me otherwise. Each day, I would sit down to meditate. My Higher Self would redirect me to one of the Three Creator Centers before I even understood what they were. The process was non-linear, spiraling between all three in its own order and timing.

I was shown over the years how these three centers are the primary centers of creation within the human body. The Sacral Center represents the Feminine, the Third Eye represents the Masculine, and the Heart represents the Child.

When all three centers are awakened, they merge back into Oneness. In ancient teachings, it is said that when this happens, humans can create entire universes. Think about that for a moment. The absolute power that is truly within you. This power doesn't arise through effort or healing. It awakens as Aliveness when you meet yourself within these centers as wholeness.

In Ecstatic Creation, this unification occurs. Here in Coherent Creation, we focus on deepening your intimacy with each center individually and then beginning to work with them as a unit.

It is important to recognize that as you work with one center, you are working with all three. The most direct way is to listen to your body and follow where your intuition guides you. Work in that center until you feel called toward another.

As you open one of the three centers, you will be opening the other two indirectly. But the intimacy is found when you spend time with each center uniquely. Just as the Feminine, Masculine, and Child each carry their own distinct quality, each Creator Center does too.

When you become intimate with them, you learn their gifts, their wisdom, and how to utilize them fully. And meeting yourself in this intimacy is the root of creation itself. Because these centers are not personal mechanisms. They are the cosmic forces of creation expressing as you.

In order for light to be created into physical form, it must become more dense. The word dense tends to trigger an association with heavy. But density and heaviness are not the same thing. Density is simply the compression of light into form.

Consider that an atom, the very building block of physical matter, is 99.9% empty space. Even at its most dense, form is primarily space. Creation gives light structure. And that structure requires polarity.

Pure energy—formless, unified, complete—splits into polarity. Masculine and Feminine. This split is the playground of density. The very condition that makes physical form possible.

The moment polarity exists, magnetism is born. Each side pulls toward the other, seeking reunion. Separation yearning to once again unite. This magnetism creates friction. And friction is where the pain of separation is felt. It is the wound that is passed down from generation to generation. One side opposing the other. It is the creative force, distorted by the belief in separation.

But when friction is met, creation returns to oneness. Where duality meets, God is revealed. And this revelation is where Aliveness is awakening. The Masculine and Feminine merge to create the Child. Creation born. You are that creation and also the creator. The Trinity, creating itself.

To actualize light into form within the human experience requires unity within the self. This is the purpose of the Three Creator Centers. They are the Trinity within your body, the mechanism through which you assist ethereal energy to become physical reality. And they are not isolated. Trinity inside of Trinity inside of Trinity, infinitely. As within, so without.

The human body is the vessel of this absolute magic. You are miraculous. And you have the power to create miracles. You only need to align the Trinity within you. And to do that, you must meet yourself in the friction of creation. To step into the fire of your own pain of separation through the conviction of your wholeness.

The Trinity within our body is the Three Creator Centers. These three centers represent the inner Feminine, inner Masculine, and inner Child. This has nothing to do with your sexual identity. Everyone has all three. Each of us will identify more naturally with one than the others, but it is the harmony of all three that awakens your Creative Genius.

The Sacral Center - The Feminine

During one particularly potent and painful meeting with my Sacral Center, the Great Mother guided me to work in my cervix. The minute I connected to it through meditation, an entire past life flashed before my eyes.

I was in a harem serving Greek royalty. A sex slave. The cool stones of the castle pressed against the soles of my feet. Silk robes brushed against my skin. I could smell bread cooking somewhere deep within the walls. And I could feel the lust of the king—fat, entitled, and absolute in his power—moving toward me like a shadow I could not outrun. He reeked of sweat and sex. A greed that could never be satiated.

I knew the performance that won the award. The moans, the movements of my body, the acts that diminished my very Aliveness yet kept me in his favor. Every moment felt dirty. Like a lie I had no power to disown. And I had learned that pleasing him well earned privileges. Better food. Softer quarters. Small mercies in a life that offered very few.

But those privileges created a chasm between the other women and me. I was not one of them. And I was not his. I belonged to no one, not even to myself. I existed in the space between, neither captive nor free, neither connected nor sovereign.

In that life, my mother of this life was also in the harem. She was my closest companion, the one thread of genuine love in a world built on transactions.

One day, something shifted in me. A rebellion stirred so deep within my body that I could not deny it. I was terrified. And yet I could no longer stay. I could no longer be a slave. What surprised me was how seductive the comfort of captivity was; the known, however diminishing, almost felt more charming than the terrifying idea of sovereignty. But I could not remain in a world where I had never truly belonged.

I turned to my friend. I begged her to come with me. She refused.

I left anyway. And the freedom I found was nothing like I had imagined. I was starving, running in fear, always listening for the sound of pursuit. The guilt of leaving her behind moved through me like a wound that wouldn't close. I had chosen myself. And it had cost me the only love I had known in that life.

I worked with this past life for weeks. Layers upon layers of sexual and emotional trauma moved out of my cervix. It felt deeply personal and yet ancestral, as if I were clearing not just one life but a lineage. The weight of chains pressing down through generations. Lifetimes of suppression screaming through that single life.

Then one day, while doing something entirely mundane, picking up the house, my phone rang. It was my father.

My mother had been diagnosed with cervical cancer. Aggressive. No warning. It had appeared seemingly out of nowhere.

The moment he said the words, my cervix lit up with the exact pain I had been working with for weeks. As if I had called its name. Emotions from a past life rippled through my body. A knowing that preceded any logic.

I was shocked. And yet, I was not.

I could see it all. I had been working in the very energies that had created the cancer. Her own pain from that life, the slavery of her body, a bitter betrayal that had never fully healed. In this life, she had suppressed much of her desire for that very reason. Unmet moments of Aliveness, bound by the belief of separation, had settled into the body as disease. The body holds everything. And sometimes, what we carry in our cells is not only ours.

My mother is now in remission. When I told her everything—the past life, the harem, the escape, the guilt of leaving her behind—she said very little. But I felt her body register. Her mind could not connect to the story, and I did not expect it to. Without the experience, it is like being told someone else's dream. But the body knows. Hers did. And somewhere beneath the words, she recognized what I was carrying for her.

The cervix is a stargate, connecting the ethereal with the physical. The female body is the vessel of creation. The inner Feminine, no matter the body you inhabit, is the receptive essence. She is the void, the nothingness from which all of creation emerges. She is the dark before the light. The womb before birth. In her truest nature, she is pure creative power.

She Is Power

Strength is masculine. Power is feminine.

The Feminine is pure creative power. In a single moment, she can create life. Gaia shows us this. A volcano erupts, and new land is born from nothing. A forest burns, and new growth emerges from the ash. She breathes, and creation simply is.

That same creative power also destroys. Cycles of death and rebirth. Energy is recycled and born anew. With each series, creation expands and then contracts.

Ebbs and then flows. Like the tides of the ocean, shifting throughout the year.

The womb expresses this exact process every month. The bleed is the shed, the destruction, the release of what is no longer valid for creation. The emotional residue of the cycle, unexpressed, unmet, unprocessed, and the creative potential that was never given form.

When a woman does not know how to release, to surrender to the cycle, the body attempts to release it in other ways. Reproductive issues and PMS are often suppressed emotions and creative energy. Just like the story of my mother.

For those without a womb, the moon cycle offers the same invitation. The Feminine within all of us moves in cycles of creation and release. To resist that rhythm is to resist creation itself. Surrendering to death fully is what awakens Aliveness within.

The womb is a physical container directly connected to the Cosmic Womb. The void. The no-thing. Pure potentiality awaiting the spark of creation. In the void, there is neither nothing nor anything. It is beyond form. It is the space from which all creation is born.

The womb has not been revered as she deserves. My story, and my mother's story, are not unique. They are the echo of generations of women who carried the weight of this misunderstanding in their bodies. When we begin to revere her, we begin to revere creation itself.

The Sacral Center governs our sexual energy, our creative life force energy, and our emotional body. It is also the seat of our Shakti. Most teachings place Shakti at the root, and I honor that. What I have been shown by the Great Mother and confirmed through direct experience is that her consciousness is governed by the sacral. This distinction matters less than the relationship you build with her.

As you deepen your relationship with the Sacral Center, you will begin to feel her stir. Shakti awakens here. And as she does, everything the sacral governs—your sexual energy, your creative fire, your emotional body—begins to move with her.

Shakti. Emotion. Sex.

The Sacral Center is the source of creative life force energy.

It is where creation lives in the body before it becomes anything. Before the idea, before the action, before the form—the energy of creation gathers here. It is the womb of your reality.

It governs three primary energies within you, each essential to the act of creation.

The first is Shakti, the creative life force itself. According to Hindu philosophy, the seat of Kundalini Shakti has not always been fixed. In earlier yugas, more spiritually evolved epochs, her seat resided in the sacral. The theory suggests that as humanity descended in consciousness, so did she, to the root chakra. The Great Mother has always taught me that her consciousness is governed by the sacral, and that as we evolve, we return her home.

The second is the emotional body. Emotions are energy in motion, the language of the creative life force moving through you. When emotions are expressed and released, creative energy flows. When they are suppressed, stored, or unmet, that same energy becomes stagnant. It has nowhere to go. This is why emotional health is not separate from creative health. They are the same current. What you feel, you create with. And what you refuse to feel, you create from anyway, fragmented, from the wound of separation.

This is also why all great art elicits emotion, because it was created from emotion as emotion.

We have not been taught to work with our emotions. Our parents, our society, and our culture have largely shut down the emotional body in favor of logic and productivity. But shutting down the emotional body is shutting down creative life force itself. Just as Tim had experienced when he lost Oliver.

The third is your sexual energy and the organs that govern it. The ovaries and testes are not simply reproductive organs. They are creative instruments of extraordinary intelligence.

Within both, there are two distinct creative energies at work, expressed as polarity.

The receptive nature, held in the left ovary or left testicle, is your inner muse. It is the energy of receiving, of replenishing, of allowing beauty, sensuality, and creative inspiration to move through you. This is the energy that says, take a bath, daydream, get dressed up for no reason other than the joy of it. It sounds indulgent. It is essential. This energy sustains the spirit and ultimately fuels all external creative works. When you dismiss it as frivolous, you cut off the source of your creative replenishment. The muse goes quiet. The well runs dry.

The projective nature, held in the right ovary or right testicle, is your inner explorer. The one who says, "Let's ride." This is the energy that takes what has been received, what has been dreamed and felt and gathered, and moves it outward into the world. It is bold. It is directional. It carries your creative spirit into physical form. Your offering is essential. Make your voice heard. Begin your work.

Together, these two energies complete the creative cycle of the Sacral Center. Receive and replenish. Gather and express. Without both, creation is incomplete. One who only receives becomes stagnant. One who only projects becomes depleted. The harmony of both is the rhythm of creative Aliveness.

As you deepen your relationship with the Sacral Center, you will begin to feel her stir. Shakti awakens here. And as she does, everything the sacral governs—your sexual energy, your creative fire, your emotional body—begins to move with her.

Meet the Mother

Start by taking three deep, cleansing breaths into your body. Breathe fully. Breathe completely. Breathe into the I AM state. Feel it activate through your body. Now drop your awareness to your Sacral Center. Move into a state of presence. Place your hand over your Sacral Center. Feel the touch of your hand against your abdomen. Feel the movement of the breath in your body.

Now deepen your breath. Breathe down into this center. Fill it with your breath. And notice what arises. What do you feel? What do you see or experience? Meet yourself here in this moment. Allow the experience to simply unfold. Allow the wisdom of your body to guide you.

Feel the Great Mother, Gaia, the earth beneath your body. Feel your body and being connect to her. Can you receive her? Can you commune with her? Breathe as if you are breathing Her. When you do this, you might feel your womb/hara light up. Soften your body deeply in her presence. Allow the Great Mother to meet you in this moment. Meet her as Her.

If you wish, you can breathe directly into your womb or hara. Or into each ovary or testicle separately. Move your breath around here. Get up and move if you feel called. Or rock your pelvis back and forth to support the body.

Is there a word, sound, or tone that desires to be expressed from your womb/hara? Or your pelvis? Does the primal energy of the feminine desire to speak through you?

Now bring your desire into your womb. Hold your awareness on your womb with the intention of your desire. Breathe into that. What does your desire want to express? A sound? A word? Meet your desire as the I AM in your womb/hara. Can you feel the ache? Can you breathe into and allow it?

Does your body want to move? What expression is the fullness of your desire from the womb/hara? Breathe here. Allow. Notice what arises. Allow Aliveness to awaken as you meet the emotions, feelings, and experiences in the I AM state.

Move, dance, sing, feel, express. Be the wildness of your desire expressing into physical form. Be the energy of creation in the here and now. As you meet yourself here, you are your desire.

Stay here fully. When you feel ready, soften back into stillness. Hold the I AM and simply feel your body. When ready, write down what you experienced.

This exercise is everything. While it might seem very simple, it will, over time, reveal all that you need to deeply know yourself here. And there are other ways to support and nourish your Sacral Center.

Tend the Flame

All the creative arts activate the Sacral Center. It isn't about how good you are at any of them. It is about utilizing them the way a child does. Free. Open. Without judgment. Think of a young child when they first learn to draw; they scribble. Just straight lines back and forth in whatever color they choose. That level of authenticity is what allows children their creative expression. They aren't doing it for anyone but themselves.

Let yourself paint, sing, dance, or draw as a direct expression of how you feel in this moment. That is all. Feelings expressed through the arts. Creation moving through you as you. When you create, you are not just making something. You are learning the language of your own creative life force. How does it feel in your body when it moves through you? Whether it speaks to you through sound, images, words, or feeling. This is how you become intimate with it. This is how you begin to recognize it when it stirs.

This is communion with creation within.

What feels closest to you right now in this moment? Not what you are best at. But what beckons you to play? Your creative expression could be through writing, drawing, coloring, puzzles, makeup, fashion, decorating, music, or gardening. There are infinite ways in which your creative spirit can come through you.

Let creation show you the dance. All you have to do is be willing to be led, guided by love. Meeting yourself in the moment when you judge your creations, when you feel inferior, when you struggle to know what to do. Meet yourself and allow Aliveness to awaken.

The last activator of this center is sexual exploration and intimacy. When sexual energy is aligned with the heart, something extraordinary occurs. Two Creator Centers open simultaneously. This is the beginning of what the ancients called sexual magic, which can be explored further once your Aliveness awakens in the Sacral Center.

You don't need a partner to work with your sexual power. Sometimes it is even more beneficial to begin with your own energy. It takes focus to master your own sexual energy, let alone combine it with another's.

Orgasm is ecstatic energy. An incredibly high vibration. Not all orgasms open the chakras, and not all orgasms are ecstatic. But when it is, it is one of the most powerful tools available to you for accessing the energies of the Sacral Center.

The beautiful opportunity that sexual exploration offers is intimacy. Intimacy with yourself or intimacy with another. Intimacy with self means spending presence with your body. Feeling it. Acknowledging what you feel and how certain touches, strokes, and movements feel to you. Noticing any triggers that arise when you bring awareness to certain areas of your body.

Intimacy means holding space for all the thoughts and emotions that arise as you meet yourself here. Allowing yourself to feel them, love and accept yourself for them, and ultimately move into a space of deep honor of your body and of self.

That is intimacy. Without it, the Sacral Center will never allow its true brilliance to be revealed. When we are unable to be vulnerable with ourselves, we create protection. The only thing that protection does is hold in your own genius. And you built that protection for good reason. Meeting it with love is what releases it.

This is an invitation to sexual exploration. To meet yourself there, in that tender and powerful space.

Working with your sexual energy means being fully present with yourself or with yourself and your partner. Breathe into your body. Meet yourself there in all the sensations. Both pleasure and discomfort. Let your body move, let your body express itself. What primal energy wishes to rise here? A roar? Perhaps even a gentle bite on your love? When I am in my full primal expression, my teeth desire to make contact with his skin. I don't bite hard. No need. It is the action that matters.

Maybe you desire to rock your hips, stroke your body. Let go of the need for orgasm. Bring in the energy of exploration and play. Be wondrous at what can be experienced when orgasm stops being the end goal.

I do recommend having a conversation with your partner beforehand so that they understand your desire for exploration. Ensure that communication is clear and safe for both of you to be fully present and available to this energy.

You have just touched the root of your creative fire. Now let it rise.

The Heart Center - The Child

Jessica came to me, frustrated and confused. She had experienced a string of failed relationships. Not men who cheated or behaved badly, but men who simply left. Always for someone else. She could see the pattern clearly, but she didn't understand why it was happening.

She desperately desired a life partner. She was tired of watching movies alone, laughing or crying with no one beside her. Tired of travels that lacked another person to enjoy them, the void that stood next to her in every photograph. She didn't want to live alone. And she certainly didn't want to die alone.

When I dropped into her energy, I immediately knew that she needed to forgive. But as I told her this, I watched her mouth turn down slightly, her shoulders giving a small shrug. She said she honestly didn't feel any ill feelings toward anyone. No dramatic trauma, no deep resentment.

She said that she had actively forgiven every single man she had been with. Who was left to forgive?

But despite her apprehension, Jessica agreed to give it a shot. We created a daily practice of forgiveness. Over the next few weeks, nothing happened. "I don't feel that this is accomplishing anything," she told me politely. But she continued to devote herself to it.

Months passed. And then one day, in her own quiet practice, a memory surfaced that she had no recollection of. She was a little girl in a large department store with her father and brother. One minute she turned around, and they were gone. She looked everywhere. Her father was nowhere to be found.

In reality, it was only for a moment. A small, forgettable moment by any adult measure. But to her, as a child in that moment, it had felt as if she had been swallowed up by the store and everything in it. It had felt like complete abandonment.

As the memory came into her awareness, her entire body lit up, and her heart clamped down. Shut. In that single forgotten moment lived the belief that had shaped every relationship that followed. Her father left. Men leave. I am someone who gets left behind.

It was a profound realization as the puzzle completed itself. It was as if the heart had been protecting itself all these years. Like a valiant soldier protecting the queen.

Except the queen felt stranded and alone rather than protected and dignified.

Jessica realized that she was the one who had abandoned herself all those years. Shut down her own heart and then blamed everyone else. And she chose forgiveness. She chose to meet herself in the pain, from wholeness, from sovereignty.

And then life offered her something she didn't expect.

Her father fell gravely ill with aggressive pancreatic cancer. Instead of a new relationship arriving, Jessica found herself at his bedside. Supporting him. Present with him in his final moments. She felt her heart meet her father's heart. She felt the feeling of love that she had been numb to for so many years. Even in the sadness of his last few moments, her heart was able to remain open. Loving and joyous.

She said it felt like coming home.

About a year after we had ceased our sessions, she wrote to me. She had met someone. The void in the photographs was filled. The presence of another's laughter filled the living room walls. And for the first time, she told me, it felt different. Like she was being chosen. With a certainty of the heart that needed no explanation.

Jessica chose to meet herself even though she couldn't feel the wound. Nothing obvious to point to. Nothing that made sense to the mind. But forgiveness is magical like that. It doesn't need a direction. It knows the way of the Heart.

That magic is the Child.

Love That Binds

The Child is not just your inner child. It is *the* Child. The Great Child. The Divine Child. The neutral principle of creation—the innocence, the coherence, the stabilizing center that holds the polarity without collapsing into it.

In the atom, the Child is represented by the neutron. The neutron is neutral. Still. It is the nuclear cement that holds the entire structure together without moving. Simply through its existence, it stabilizes the atom.

That stabilization allows creation to move without wobbling. Without instability. It means the movement is no longer distorted by reactivity or resistance. From neutrality, movement is clear. The pendulum of polarity can swing full force, anchored in stillness. That swing is the friction of creation.

The Child is the anchor point between the Masculine and the Feminine. Without the Child, the Masculine and Feminine are simply charge and orbit, beautiful, powerful, and unstable. The Child is what allows the Trinity to cohere.

The Child has another important role: the pause.

In the breath, between inhalation and exhalation, there is a moment of complete stillness. No movement and no change. That is the Child. That is the changelessness experienced through the body.

Most of us have been taught to value movement. The inhale. The exhale. The doing and the undoing. But it is the space between that holds everything together coherently. Without it, breath is just motion. With it, breath becomes the Trinity itself.

We have largely forgotten the natural cycles of creation. Each cycle is essential. You cannot only flow. That is the energy of force, not power.

Stillness is not emptiness. Think of deep winter, after the trees have pulled the nutrients from their leaves and everything has fallen to the ground. Nothing appears to be happening. And yet, beneath the surface, everything is being processed, integrated, and prepared for what comes next. After the expansion of the masculine flow state, tremendous information and change have moved through. The body, mind, and spirit need time to integrate them.

That is the cycle of the Child.

Without integration, the changes don't stick. And without stillness, change becomes chaotic, and the force between the push and pull becomes conflict. An internal fight between the two polarities.

But our minds don't like stillness. It is up to you to train your mind to be still. Your mind is a powerful tool, but left to its own devices, it will manically think about all kinds of things throughout the day, hemorrhaging the very creative energy it was meant to serve.

Learn to direct the mind, utilizing the Key of Presence. Initially, your mind will become even more active. But the more you connect to this stillness, the more you begin to prefer it.

From here, your relationship to each polarity becomes clearer and more powerful. The Masculine moves with more precision. The Feminine flows with more trust. Because the Child holds them both without collapsing into either.

Aliveness awakens where you meet the attachment and even addiction to movement, change, and distraction. And that anchor of the Child is the intelligence of the Heart Center. The heart sits at the center of the Three Creator Centers. Between the sacral, the seat of the gross body and creative life force, and the Third Eye, the seat of the subtle body and sovereign vision. It is the nucleus between the two poles. The coherence that makes the polarity generative.

Soul Blueprint. Coherence. Union.

The Heart Center is the center of coherence. It is the command center of creation.

It governs three primary aspects within you, each essential to the act of creation.

The first is the Soul blueprint. The heart is where our Soul blueprint is located. When we become fully present to the energy of the heart, we merge into Oneness. Our egos dissolve into the background, and only being-ness remains.

It is through this purity of existence that our Soul's desires are revealed to us.

Your desires are not random. They are the Soul's precise navigation system, pointing you toward the exact energies within yourself that are ready to be met, incorporated, and transcended. Each one is a breadcrumb back to a fragment of the Soul waiting to be received.

We must only feel its truth and trust in the intelligence of Source.

And that trust begins with understanding what the heart is actually navigating toward. Karma is separation desiring to be met. This can be individual karma of your Soul, ancestral, or collective karma.

Your Genius does not live outside of your
wounds. It lives within them,
waiting to be retrieved.

When we experience trauma that we do not process, no matter the size, a portion of the Soul becomes entrapped in that moment. Karma awaiting unification. Held in the amber of an unmet experience, carrying the wisdom of what that moment had to offer.

Soul retrieval happens in the heart. It is the portal through which these frozen fragments are met, received, and returned home. When we meet the karma and unresolved trauma with forgiveness, those parts of the Self integrate back into wholeness. We receive the golden nugget of wisdom that the experience was always holding for us.

Karma is the Soul circling back to the moments that still hold a part of it frozen, offering another opportunity to meet, retrieve, and return to wholeness. The more you allow your wounding to be met with love, the more of your own unique brilliance you will discover and embody. Your genius does not live outside of your wounds. It lives within them, waiting to be retrieved.

The second is coherence. The heart is not simply an emotional center. It is an intelligence center. The heart has its own neural network, its own brain. It sends more signals to the brain than the brain sends to it. Which raises the question: which one is truly in charge?

The heart's electromagnetic field is the largest in the body, extending several feet beyond the physical form. It is constantly communicating with every cell, every system, broadcasting the vibrational truth of what you are creating. Not what you think you are creating. What you are actually creating.

Governing this field is the thymus gland, known in spiritual traditions as the higher heart. The seat of the Soul. It bridges the physical body with the emotional and spiritual realms, governing unconditional love, compassion, and divine connection. When the heart is open and the thymus is activated, the entire field comes into coherence. Every system aligns. Creation flows without resistance.

The third is union. When you meet yourself in your desires, you bring the energy of unconditional love to the very places that have been in separation. That love unifies the fragments. And unification is transcendence. This is how the heart transcends karma. Through the courageous act of following what it most deeply desires.

In the heart, the pull is to merge back into the innocence of the Child. Just as a man and woman seek each other out to create a family. A unit.

Here, we experience creation as a family. One. We naturally desire to serve through our genius, knowing that it benefits the highest good of all.

The heart allows us to connect to others beyond the differences of the mind. Beyond culture, belief, and the many expressions of separation that divide us. From the heart, we accept the various forms and expressions of creation. Compassion arises effortlessly and naturally as an extension of grace.

The union of the heart and the womb crosses time and space.

For women, when the heart is lit up vibrationally within its desires, the womb responds in the delicious energy of yearning. Yearning, within this context, is the pure desire of the womb to create the heart's desires.

The womb will light up in yearning and thus activate the incredible mechanisms of the womb's creative process. Part of this process is magnetism. The womb is the magnetic energy of a woman. And when it is activated in yearning, it begins to magnetize energy to it in great magnitudes. The woman can actually feel her womb vibrating with a yearning energy that is directly connected to and serving the heart's desires.

For men, your heart can activate the creative life force energy within you. While this will not feel like the yearning a woman feels in the womb, make no mistake about your power to create.

And yet, beneath all of this power, all of this cosmic intelligence, lives something far more tender. The most profound expression that the Child gifts us is the return to our own innocence.

We are innately innocent beings. From our core, we do not desire to create pain, hatred, or cause ourselves or anyone else harm. We desire love, acceptance, and the joy of creation.

When we believe that we are not loved or lovable, we begin to create a life that reflects that.

We protect our hearts. This might be expressed outwardly with aggression toward others, or this could be expressed internally by shutting down through shame and guilt.

In order to return to our innocence, we must meet separation in our hearts. We must meet the betrayal, the grief, the guilt, and the shame. As we meet it from wholeness, as the I AM, Aliveness is awakened and the innocence of the Child returns.

When the innocence of the Child is restored, the coherence of the field is restored. This coherence stops the destructive forces that duality alone generates. Those destructive forces are the wound of separation expressing itself.

The Masculine and Feminine without the Child are generative but unstable. The Feminine creates and destroys in equal measure, cycling endlessly, unable to cohere into form. The Masculine forces and consumes, requiring constant fuel from the outside because nothing is being generated from within. Two poles seeking union but unable to find it because coherence is not present.

Through the Child, the coherence of Creation is remembered, realized, and thus experienced. It was never not there, only forgotten. The world, once again, appears like a playground. Curiosity expands each moment into a glorious journey. Wonder gifts the unfamiliar as something to rejoice in instead of fear. We create from the pure expression and joy of our Creative Genius.

It is slightly paradoxical that we must accept who we are and what we are creating in order to create something new. But that is the Child. Paradoxical, magical, miraculous.

Being centered in the heart is to be unstoppable. For all is seen as love.

Meet the Child

As we enter this connection session, invite innocence in. Simply through your intention. Take a few full breaths into your heart as you allow the innocence of the Heart to guide you here in this moment.

Feel the breath in your heart. Let the breath fill you here. Fill your heart with innocence. Observe what arises as you do this. You can place your hands over your heart or wrap your arms around yourself in a hug. What touch feels nourishing to you here and now?

As you breathe into the heart, imagine the portal, infinite, into Soul, into Oneness. Breathe into that portal. Breathe into the I AM state. Feel the vastness of that presence here. What do you notice?

Meet yourself from the I AM state, as it is. And breathe. What do you feel? What sensations arise? What images or thoughts emerge? You can also tap here, over your heart. Tap in a rhythmic manner. Let the rhythm draw you deeper.

What wishes to be expressed here? A word. A tone. Perhaps a song. Let your heart speak. Let the Child express.

Now bring your desire into your heart. Feel its presence, held by the I AM state. Held by the innocence. Held by love. Allow the desire to rest in the heart as you breathe. Meet yourself here fully. Meet what arises. Meet the sensations, the thoughts.

Breathe into your heart. Feel as your breath meets your body. As you, in the I AM state, meet all that is held there. All is wished to be held there. What does your desire wish to bring forth in this moment? Does it wish to express, move, or simply be? Notice what arises naturally from your desire, held in your heart by the I AM state.

Allow Aliveness to awaken as you meet the emotions, feelings, and experiences with wholeness. As wholeness.

From here, invite yourself into play. Don't overthink it; let the Child lead. Play is allowance. Play is presence. When we are playful, we are allowing the moment to unfold for itself.

What does play look like for you right now? In this moment? It could be the smallest of gestures or hours of exploration. When you are complete, write down what you experienced.

Nourishment That Serves

Forgiveness is often seen as an act toward another. But forgiveness rarely has anything to do with another, even when the experience involved another person.

We can hold a great deal of resentment toward ourselves for the choices that we have made. Even when someone directly hurts us, the core is usually the finger pointed at ourselves. We know, deep within our hearts, that we should have, could have chosen, and created differently.

Especially for trauma that happened in our childhood. Children are quick to blame themselves. And that blame solidifies throughout our adult lives.

However, because self-blame is immensely painful, we project that pain outward onto others. It gives us a sense of entitlement and victory when the truth is that we deeply long to surrender to our own misgivings.

Any time we feel blame toward another, the root is the self.

Forgiveness is the antidote to this confusing and distorted pattern. It begins with yourself. For everything you have ever created or acted upon. For what you understood and for what you could not yet see. When you forgive yourself fully, forgiveness naturally spreads to all who were part of the experience.

Forgive yourself, and your heart will open. Forgive yourself, and you will naturally forgive others. Forgive yourself, and the feelings of compassion, joy, and love will return to your heart.

Forgiveness does not mean that you continue any relationship in your life. You can forgive someone and never speak to them again. It also does not mean that you condone their actions.

Instead, forgiveness releases you from the timeline of the wound. In the quantum realm, it releases the entanglement with that other Soul. Resentment and blame attach us to the Soul of the being who harmed us. Vibrationally bound until forgiveness releases us.

If someone has truly harmed you, forgive them and trust the intelligence of karma. The universe always seeks harmony and equilibrium.

Forgive and set yourself free. Forgive and meet the wound with wholeness. And there, Aliveness awakens.

Boundaries are another powerful way to nourish and open the Heart Center.

Self-love starts with boundaries. To me, boundaries are self-integrity. Boundaries are as simple as asking, "Is this loving to self?"

This question gifts you an immediate answer. Boundaries are not mental rules and regulations. Created that way, they cannot honor the dynamism of your being or the fullness of any given experience.

You might be with one person, and when you ask if it is loving to yourself, you hear no. Then you could be in what seems like the same experience with another person, and when you ask, you receive a yes. That is dynamic integrity. Present to the moment, not the idea or concept of the moment.

There is always more present in any moment than the mind can perceive. When we create rigid rules and regulations, we are attempting to control life rather than trust our inner wisdom and wholeness.

I often find that when people talk about boundaries, they are actually speaking to creating walls of protection around themselves. Walls don't keep anything out and only suppress our own sovereignty and Creative Genius. The most powerful way to create your reality is to vibrate at the energy of love. It is an act of valor to live as love. That valor is the most magnetic energy available to humanity.

When we choose love, we emanate love. A vibration that alchemizes whatever it touches. Hatred, fear, separation, met by love, awakens Aliveness. This is the power of ecstatic energy. In the rapture of love, everything becomes Aliveness.

Love yourself so completely that nothing can trigger you or hurt you. That is the field of love made sovereign.

Practice asking yourself, "Is this loving to self?" and taking direct action on what you hear. The answer knows where to go. Your only task is to follow it. If you receive a no and you do it anyway, you further validate your belief that you are not worthy of love.

If you hear yes, and you do not take that action, you equally validate that belief.

To live with an open heart is the most courageous thing that we can do. To meet life without walls. To trust your inner wisdom over the comfort of control. That is the boundary of love. That is self-integrity lived.

The Third Eye Center - The Masculine

I was standing in a stall with my arm on the back of a beautiful black mare. She was so relaxed that her head was practically lying on the floor. I was working on her both energetically and physically.

She was carrying a great deal of emotional trauma in her body. Her owner had hired me to help her work through it. She had been abused and didn't trust humans easily. You could see it in her eyes, an apprehension of an animal that knows the harm humans can inflict. A tension held in her body that is ready, at any moment, to flee or fight.

She was a stoic mare, the type that doesn't want to show any vulnerability. When I first met her, she stood proud. She didn't flinch or give any signal that she was receiving me at all. This was our second session. After only one, her body had softened, and she had begun to trust me.

As I worked, I felt an intuitive nudge. A presence at the edge of my awareness. My Higher Self informed me that Archangel Raphael desired to help her.

This was early on in my spiritual journey. I was meditating daily and had just started to connect to the Archangels. I didn't really know much about them, let alone know how to work with them.

But with deep honor, I called Archangel Raphael in. In my mind's eye, I saw an emerald green light fill the space, like steam in a sauna. The energy felt nourishing and soft. Then two white wings appeared.

At this point, my mind stepped in. "You are making this up. This is just in your head." My mind often rejected what I experienced in those days. I had learned young to distrust what I saw.

I looked down at the mare. Her lower lip was dangling from her face as if it were about to fall off. Her eyes were closed. I watched as the wings moved over her, and just as they touched her withers, her head shot straight up.

Her eyes were wide. Her ears pointed back toward the wings that now rested on her shoulders. She licked and chewed, a sign of release in horses, and immediately dropped her head back down.

I was shocked. There had been no noise. No movement. My hands hadn't moved an inch. The only thing that had happened was Archangel Raphael's wings touching her withers. And her reaction had been perfectly timed with the exact moment of contact.

I then watched as the muscles in her shoulders went into spasms. This often happens when energy enters an area that has been blocked, as if tiny electrodes were firing beneath the skin.

After a minute or two, the mare gave a full-body shake. Then a massive yawn, her eyes rolling back in her head. In the equine bodywork world, the shake, the yawn, and especially the eye roll all signal a significant physical release.

My mind had no logical explanation. None.

And in that moment, something shifted deep in my heart. It brought me back to my early childhood. To the beings I could see and talk to that my family called my imaginary friends. Beings of light. Guides. Angels. The same quality of presence I had just witnessed in that stall. The same energy I had just seen with my own mind's eye.

The dismissal of their existence had lived quietly in my heart until this moment. As a child, after hearing "they aren't real" over and over, I began to doubt myself.

I felt ashamed of speaking to them.

I loved their presence and felt called to spend time with them. But the shame caused me to only speak to them in secret, when no one was around. Until one day, sitting in my horse's field with them, I felt the shame rise up so strongly that I made a decision. I told myself I had to stop acting this way. I was ten years old. "Stop being a child," my mind yelled at me.

I shut it down. Convinced that it was childish. Imaginary.

And here I was, decades later, standing in a stall with another horse. The same animals that were present when I closed the gift, now present as it returned to me.

My own body reacted, much like the mare. A release of the pain of believing I had made it all up, moving through me. And my heart lit up with forgiveness. My spine straightened as if the realization itself made me stand taller.

He Who Holds

What I saw was always real. That is the gift of the Third Eye Center, and the teaching of the Masculine within you.

The Masculine is the Great Father. The downward intelligence that descends to meet the Feminine's upward power. The Mother rises from below. The Father descends from above. And the Child lives within, where they unify.

He is the structure of intelligence. Consciousness. The living, dynamic framework that gives the feminine power direction and form. With discernment, he creates the clarity needed for action.

In fact, the river made the riverbed. She
carved him through
the act of her own flow.

He is the hands that hold creation into being. The word manipulate—so long associated with control and harm—comes from the Latin manus, hand, and plere, to fill. To manipulate, in its truest sense, is to fill his hands with her creative life force energy. To give the Feminine fullness of expression. That is the Divine Masculine, the one who holds.

His role is to channel her desire, her yearning, her magnetic pull toward form. Just like the riverbed channels the river. The riverbed holds the river's power without ever owning it.

In fact, the river made the riverbed. She carved him through the act of her own flow. He was shaped by her power, her movement, her insistence on finding her way. He holds devotion to her magnitude.

Over time, in moments of great flow, the riverbed shifts. He remolds himself to meet her new form. Her wild, chaotic desire always disrupting form to recreate anew. This is how the Masculine holds structure without rigidity.

Rigidity is attachment. It limits the freedom of the Feminine. But without structure, without the riverbed, the river doesn't go anywhere. It would flood a meadow, become stagnant, and then diseased. She would lack the direction needed to return to the ocean, Creation.

The logical mind can become deeply rigid when it believes that it is the creator. This distortion leads to force, not power.

Vision. Focus. Discernment.

The Third Eye Center is the architect of creation.

It governs three primary aspects within you, each essential to the act of creation.

The first is vision and projection. The Third Eye is governed by the pineal and pituitary glands. It reads subtle light and information that exists beyond physical density.

Subtle is not created from dense. Dense is created via subtle. Think of an atom and how many atoms it takes to create your physical body. Your physical body does not create the atoms. The subtle creates the physical. And the Third Eye reads the subtle. This means it is not reading the surface of reality. It is reading the source of it.

Subtle information includes thoughts, feelings, potentials, probabilities, timeline alignments, quantum entanglements, and so much more. It isn't about psychic abilities. It is about reading the universal stream of consciousness. It is being tapped into the plethora of information that is continuously moving through the moment.

Just as the womb is always connected to the Cosmic Womb, the mind is connected to the universal intelligence through the Third Eye. It is superintelligence.

The human mind is a remarkable instrument, but it is also finite. The universe is infinite, vast, and all-knowing. The Third Eye is the bridge between the two. When you open your Third Eye and begin to engage with consciousness in this way, you begin to access information that you had no idea existed or access abilities that you never had before.

Far exceeding book smarts, diplomas, or any intelligence learned from one human to the next, the Third Eye grants you the power to tap directly into intelligence itself. All the great geniuses of the world were tapped into this direct stream of consciousness. That is why they created what they did.

Just as there is no limit to what the womb and heart can create together, there is no limit to the intelligence that the Third Eye can connect to. It is a very invigorating and delightful place to play if you enjoy intelligence.

But the Third Eye does not only receive. It also projects. It casts light, the frequencies of your imagination, into the holographic reality. Your imagination is your ability to connect to different timelines and potentialities. The brain and body do not know the difference between a strongly imagined reality and physical reality. They respond in the same way.

Projection through the Third Eye is not forced visualization. This is an important distinction from manifestation techniques. Aligned vision arises from wholeness. When you project from the wound, you create more wound. When you project from wholeness, you create from truth.

You are always projecting. The only question is what you are choosing to project. The Third Eye is both your receiver and your projector.

The second is focus. Focus is the direction of the light that is both received and projected. Just like a movie screen that you watch, you are focused on the light that is streaming into your Third Eye. And also like a movie screen, the projector is focusing a stream of light onto the screen.

The more powerful your focus, the more powerfully you can create your reality. It is imperative to cultivate both.

Without focus, the light of creation is not directional. Much like the river that floods the meadow, unfocused light spreads everywhere and lands nowhere. Think of the difference between a floodlight and a laser. Both are light. But a laser, focused to a single point, can cut through steel. That is the Masculine's gift to creation, directed light. Directed arrow.

Worry is the distortion of focus. It is focus turned against itself. Locked onto what you don't desire, feeding it with attention and vibration until it solidifies into your reality. We visualize the outcome we fear, trigger our bodies with it, and begin to vibrate in the exact energies we are trying to avoid. If you find yourself worrying, the invitation is not to stop thinking. It is to redirect your focus toward what you actually desire to create.

Discernment is the third aspect. Discernment is the Masculine's intelligence applied to the field. It is knowing which arrow to release and when. It is the ability to distinguish between the voice of the Higher Self and the voice of the wound. Between intuition and fear. Between aligned vision and projection from separation.

Where contemplation and logic meet, discernment is born. Contemplation opens the Masculine to the full field, all angles, all potentials, all information available. Logic then applies intelligence to what has been received.

When we use discernment, we are in clarity of choice. And from that clarity, the correct arrow reveals itself.

The distortion of the Masculine arises when logic loses its devotion to the Feminine. Rigidity of the mind can show up as stubbornness, fixation, obsession, and arrogance. In these energies, logic overtakes creativity, curiosity, and the very unknown energy of the void.

When the fear of not knowing is met from wholeness, Aliveness awakens.

The truth is, you have all the knowledge that is needed. You must only learn to be still enough, listen well, and take action on the internal wisdom that has never left you.

As you move deeper into your creative power, you will find the Masculine naturally becomes more fluid and less effortful. Not through effort, but by breathing into the Feminine and allowing her to rise to meet him.

Meet the Father

The Third Eye awakens through activation, not just awareness. This practice creates the conditions for your creative life force to rise and meet the Third Eye in its own intelligence.

Start by taking three deep breaths down into your belly. Feel your body. Breathe into the I AM state. Allow it to permeate every cell and inhabit your entire being. Bring your tongue to the roof of your mouth. Breathe here with the touch of your tongue to your mouth. Feel that sensation.

Now breathe deeply down into your pelvis for three full breaths. On the third breath, inhale and squeeze your perineum and anus. Draw your awareness up toward your Third Eye. Hold your awareness there. Hold your breath. Maintain the clench.

Once you cannot hold on any longer, relax. Take three deep, full breaths and then repeat the process.

I recommend ten rounds. Once complete, sit with your focus on your Third Eye. Tongue still on the roof of your mouth. What do you feel? What do you see? Simply observe.

At this point in the activation, bring your desire into your Third Eye. Feel its presence there as you hold it from the I AM state. What do you feel? You can ask to see your desire. What visuals come through? If any. Allow and observe. Be open to what is organic and natural. You aren't trying to see anything. You are allowing the desire to express via visuals.

Is there a sound that your desire wishes to express? The sound can activate it further. Witness any sound made from the Third Eye. Notice what arises. Breathe here.

When ready, can you connect to the Great Father here? What is his essence? If your Shakti is at your crown, you might feel the energy of the Great Father descend into your body. Can you soften and allow?

What do you feel when you receive the Great Father into your human form?

You may find that old beliefs about God, the Father, or masculine authority arise here. Honor them. They are simply the wound of the distorted Masculine seeking to be met. The Great Father, in his truest nature, is nothing like what we have been taught. He does not judge. He does not withhold. He descends in devotion to meet the Feminine's power. He is the intelligence that holds you, not the authority that controls you.

You will learn him just as you learn the Great Mother and Child. The relationship with the Trinity of Creation will continue to teach you over and over again. You will foster intimacy with each, just as you have with the Three Creator Centers. Allowing for the wisdom and gift of each archetype to deepen your communion with creation.

Surrendered Visualization

To cultivate the power of the Third Eye in the practicality of daily life, begin with this practice.

Sit comfortably. Soften your body. Let everything settle. Breathe into the I AM state and simply rest there. From that stillness, bring your awareness into your Third Eye. Ask to see an apple on a table.

Notice what arises. What color is the apple? What kind of table does it sit on? Look at the details in the image.

Hold your focus on the apple and see what happens around or to it. There are no right or wrong answers. This is your imagination. Anything and everything is correct.

The apple might shift, or the background might change. Observe as if you were watching a movie. Simply watch without it needing to mean anything.

After you have practiced this, you can begin to ask questions about your desires and receive answers.

Bring up the apple and hold your question in your awareness. Allow the apple to shift, change, or transform in response. Trust what arises.

When you are ready, come out of the visualization and write down what you saw.

The work that follows is the translation. Allow your mind to rest on what has arrived. Take it all in without rushing to understand it. The mind loves to fill in blanks and will jump to conclusions. Give it time and space instead. The translation will become clear.

After you feel that the image is complete, write down what you saw in as much detail as possible, without assigning meaning to any of it. Simply report what is. The interpretation will come later, in its own time.

Your physical reality will also continue to validate and deepen what was received. As taught in the House of Mirrors, life will speak to you in various ways to inform you further. The art here is in giving the conversation the spaciousness to reveal the deepest truth.

If you rush the process, only half-truths are received. You will know when the question has been fully answered. You will feel it in your body. Then, take action. This is where you build the relationship to this inner intelligence by listening to it.

When you hesitate or doubt, you are further validating the wound of separation. Aliveness is awakened in the moment when the unknown is faced, like the warrior, through the action of the arrow.

Both practices will activate and expand your Third Eye and its capabilities. But you can also nourish your Third Eye with a few tools. Being outside in the early morning light is a powerful activator. Some traditions teach sun gazing, but I have found that simply absorbing those early hours of light works well.

Research supports the healing properties of early morning light. I find that it stimulates my creativity, as well as it feels nourishing to my physical eyes. The "texture" of the light feels loving and warm in its hue.

The final activating exercise is Creative Injection, the deliberate feeding of your Third Eye with new input. New experiences, new perspectives, new information. Anything that expands the lens through which you see.

It can be anything that naturally excites you. Travel. Art. Music. Conversation with someone who thinks differently from you. A book that challenges what you believe. A walk in a place you have never been. Or taking a different route home.

The Third Eye feeds on novelty and openness.

I personally love to do this with a project or creation in mind. If you are writing a book or creating a program, explore what that creation would love to experience. This isn't mental; it's intuitive. It's playful and fun.

You do not try to immediately apply or understand what you have taken in. You cannot force the integration even if you try. You simply plant the seed and trust the intelligence of your field to process it.

This is the Masculine at his most evolved. Not controlling the outcome. Providing the conditions for intelligence to emerge. Feed your Third Eye generously. Then release. Trust the intelligence of what you have planted.

The Full Symphony

You have journeyed through each of the Three Creator Centers. Each one alive within you. Each one waiting to deepen its relationship with you.

Working with all three together creates a vibrational resonance that is unlike anything experienced in the individual centers alone. Powerful and simultaneously grounded and expansive. This is the Trinity in harmony.

I recommend spending time with each center individually before working with them as a Trinity. The more intimate you become with each one, the more powerfully they work together.

There is no fixed order. Your body will guide you. However, in my own practice, I find that I naturally breathe down into the Mother first. The sacral activates, and Shakti begins to stir. From there, she rises, and the heart begins to respond. The sacral and heart vibrate together, opening and expanding. Then the Father descends from above, and the Third Eye and heart begin to activate together. The full Trinity in motion.

When all three are open and in harmony, the resonance itself becomes your compass. You will begin to feel when one center is off because the harmony shifts. The body will tell you where to go.

Trinity Unified

Begin by breathing into the I AM state. Allow it to permeate every cell, every photon, every atom of your being. Rest here. Know yourself as this.

From the I AM, bring your awareness to your body. Feel the ground beneath you. Feel the weight of your body. Take three slow, full breaths. Allow your nervous system to arrive completely in this moment. Feel it naturally extend itself downward and connect to the Mother, upward to the Father. Inwards at the heart. Feel this connection. Communion. Breathe.

Now breathe down into the seat of your Shakti, just above the root. Greet her. Honor her. Breathe as if you are stoking her fire. Allow her to stir. Observe from the I AM state her movement. Breathe and allow her wisdom through you.

Breathe as Shakti begins to rise. Notice what you feel in your body. Allow her to rise. Feel her. Breathe her.

Take your awareness to your heart and breathe there as the I AM. Also, using your breath to stoke the fire of the Heart Center. Observe. Feel. Notice the two centers together. The Sacral and the Heart.

What do you feel here with both of them? What happens when you hold your awareness on both?

Now breathe into your Third Eye as the I AM. Tongue on the roof of your mouth. Stoke the fire of the Third Eye Center with your breath. Observe and feel. Is your Shakti here? Has she risen to your crown? Remember, no forcing, only observing and allowing.

Now bring your awareness to your Third Eye Center and Heart Center. What do these two feel like together? What do you observe?

Lastly, focus on all three. Are they communicating? Resonating as one? What is the quality of the connection between them?

Sit and allow.

What naturally arises from this communion? I recommend sitting for ten minutes in this space.

Breathe in circular breaths. Connect. Feel. Commune.

Now bring your desire into the Trinity. Hold it here from the I AM, in all three centers simultaneously. In the womb, in the heart, in the Third Eye. Feel how each center meets it differently. The womb feels its yearning. The heart holds it in love. The Third Eye sees it. Breathe into all three. Be the I AM. Be your desire. Be the Trinity creating itself.

Do you feel called to move? Express? Be still?

Stay here as long as your body desires. When ready, write down what you experienced.

Where is Aliveness awakening from this union?

Each time you answer that question, you meet yourself in wholeness. The journey of coming back to yourself is the journey of bringing these three aspects back into harmony. As you do, your outer reality begins to reflect that harmony back to you.

In Coherent Creation, you learn to work with each center individually and then in harmony with one another. In Ecstatic Creation, the three merge into one unified field of creative power. That merging has already begun.

Meet yourself here. In the Trinity of your own being. This is where your Creative Genius lives.

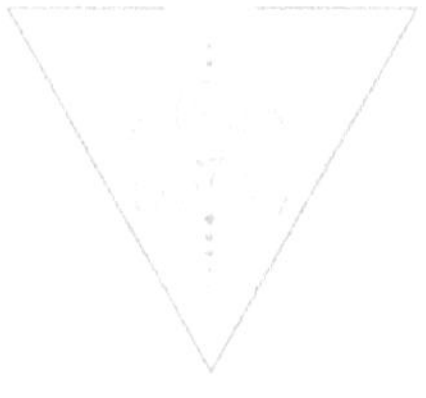

CHAPTER 9

UNIQUE GENIUS

Ethan came to me, vibrant and energetic. He was the type of person who seemed to light everyone else up around him. But there was a quality to him I couldn't quite place until we dove into the reason he was seeking support.

He was feeling an internal stir. An unsettling. But on the outside, he couldn't justify that feeling against the evidence of his life. He was good at his job. Well-respected and liked. He was reliable in the way that gets quietly rewarded—promotions he didn't ask for, responsibilities that slowly replaced his life, a title that sounded like success and felt like a sentence.

He could run systems and catch inefficiencies before anyone else saw them. He was a senior operations manager who took his job seriously, and it showed. His boss called him indispensable. His colleagues called him the fixer. And every time something broke, they gave it to Ethan.

And he fixed it. Every time.

But as he expressed to me, this gift of his, his work, his abilities, there was a flatness. Like someone who is reading lines from a play with no emotional investment. Like a man describing someone else's life. There was no Aliveness there. He was going through the motions on autopilot, and some part of him knew it.

When I pointed this out to him, he threw his head to the side as if rejecting the entire notion. "What do I have to complain about?" he said. He went on to describe all the things he had in his life. He told me the entire picture of exactly why he shouldn't want or need anything more.

He made good money. He was respected and well-liked. He had built exactly the kind of life that looked, from the outside, like enough.

And yet he was here. Because something in him knew it wasn't.

The whisper that brought him to me. The unnamed insistence that there was something more, persistent enough to make him quietly question his perfect life.

We had to go looking for that voice. And when we found it, it made complete sense.

Ethan was the oldest of three. His mother raised them alone. Without ever being told directly, he understood from a young age that he was the man of the house. That his job was to hold things together. To support. To provide. To be reliable.

There simply wasn't space to ask what he wanted. Desire in that house was not his to have. He wasn't the priority. And that belief, formed in the body of a little boy doing his best to keep everything afloat, followed him quietly into every room he had ever walked into since.

It had never been named. It lived beneath everything.

The moment we found it, his entire body softened. Like he had been holding up a building with his breath and finally gave himself permission to let go.

We met that moment from wholeness. He recognized how that was simply the boy in him who believed that. And in that instance, a huge smile lit up across his face. The innocence of a boy who was finally allowed to want something for himself.

Over a few months, we explored the subconscious beliefs that held him in an identity of the fixer. As he released that identity and met his sovereignty, his entire energy shifted.

Ironically, he became more grounded. Still with plenty of energy, but his energy felt like a wise tree rather than a jackrabbit. His genius emerged naturally. He realized that his true genius had never been in operations. It had always been people. The intimacy of feeling the truth of what was moving beneath the surface. And having the courage to name it.

He began to notice the deeper human structures that were playing out at work. Teams misaligned but pretending they weren't. People performing confidence while internally fragmented. And every time he stepped in, his instinct was to ask questions no one else was asking.

He told me how people were first taken aback. Almost as if they preferred him to simply fix the problem and keep out of their business. But his likable personality had fostered trust, and people naturally opened up. What resulted was internal transformation instead of band-aids on wounds that found other ways of festering.

Ethan told me that it felt like he was making a difference, not just solving a problem. He even said that his colleagues were telling him how he was changing their lives. He laughed and told me that, ironically, it felt so natural to him, and yet every time he experienced it, he was blown away by his own genius.

I felt the passion light up in his body. That internal flow that I feel when someone is living their genius. Magnetic and intoxicating.

The Light

Genius is not what our society has taught us it is.

We have equated the word with science, math, and creativity. With diplomas and accolades, and the rare few who seem to have been born with something the rest of us weren't. But that is not genius. That is achievement. And achievement, however impressive, is not the same thing.

Your Genius is the vibration of consciousness moving through the unique fractal of your Incarnation Blueprint. Like light through stained glass, where no two pieces are the same, no two expressions are identical.

The blueprint itself contains everything your Soul needs in this life. Your gifts. Your lessons. Your desires. The specific architecture of this incarnation, designed precisely for the expression of your Soul.

And Genius is what moves through it when the glass is clear.

This is why Genius cannot be copied, competed with, or replicated. It isn't a skill set. It isn't a profession. It isn't even a passion, though passion may point toward it. Genius is a frequency. A vibrational resonance that is so specifically, unrepeatably you, that when you are living from it, the world around you feels it. Even if they can't name what they are feeling.

Genius cannot be comprehended by the mind. The moment you try to grasp it, define it, or contain it, you narrow its expression. The mind is not the enemy here.

But it is finite. It wants to name what it holds. And Genius is by nature indefinable, boundless, and self-directing. The more fully the I AM is anchored, the more purely Genius moves through, unfiltered by the identity structures that were never actually you.

Think of the humans throughout history whose light has been undeniable. Einstein. Tesla. Mozart. Maya Angelou. Martin Luther King Jr. Michael Jordan. Frida Kahlo. Their genius was not their craft. It was the clarity of consciousness moving through them. A frequency so unique, so individual that no one in the world could ever replace or replicate them. So clear, so flowing, they couldn't stop it. They could only surrender to its brilliance.

And for every genius whose light has been witnessed by the world, there are countless others whose genius will never make headlines. The mother whose presence transforms everyone who enters her home. The teacher whose words land in a child and never leave. The builder whose hands carry a frequency of care into everything they create. Genius does not require an audience. It only requires expression.

Other people will feel the truth of it. They will resonate with it, understand it conceptually, and gain value from it as your genius serves the One. However, they can never fully understand it to the complexity and embodied level that you do because they simply are not it. And this can feel lonely.

This loneliness is a challenging aspect of your Genius, and yet, when you understand it, it can further deepen your communion with Creation. Because it is between you and Source. It is the mechanism of that relationship. It is your service to the world through that communion.

Your gifts and talents are the vessels through which your Genius moves. But they are not the Genius itself. Ethan was gifted at operations. But his Genius was the intimacy with human consciousness. The feeling, the movement. The subtleties that his genius caught, that his mind never even saw. The gift was the door. The Genius was what lived behind it.

This distinction matters because many people spend their entire lives developing their gifts and never touch their Genius. They become very good at the door without ever walking through it.

Your Genius emerges from the I AM state. It is not something you build, or achieve, or someday arrive at. It is what becomes visible when the Trinity within you—the Child, the Feminine, the Masculine—merges into Oneness. When there is no fragmentation in the glass, the light moves through pure and clear.

Genius is not a destination. It is a
frequency you inhabit more and more fully
as you awaken the aliveness within.

No refraction. Direct flow of light through the vessel of your human form.

This is why the work of this entire book has been pointing here. Every moment of meeting yourself. Every choice of sovereignty over separation. Every breath taken in presence rather than performance. All of it has been clearing the glass.

And the world receives something it has
never received before. You.

Genius is not a destination. It is a frequency you inhabit more and more fully as you awaken the Aliveness within. As Aliveness awakens, you anchor deeper into wholeness. As you anchor into wholeness, the light of your Higher Self emerges more fully into human form.

And the world receives something it has never received before.

You.

Your Genius feels like coming home. It is coming home to yourself.

But the path there is rarely straight.

Following the Signal Home

I left the United States at nineteen with no plan. I knew only one thing: travel lit me up. So I said yes and boarded a plane for the first time in my life, bound for Fiji. I had no plan beyond the destination. I didn't arrive with a career mapped out or a vision for what my life would become. I arrived with a backpack and a willingness to follow the signal.

I planned to dive while I was traveling. What I hadn't planned was that diving would become my life for the next six years. It literally fell into my lap. The moment I discovered I could work in diving and travel simultaneously, everything aligned. I became a dive instructor and spent years living on islands and abroad, teaching people to breathe underwater and feel the vastness of the ocean floor.

I traveled from location to location, easily finding work and a transient community of instructors and divers who moved from island to island as I did. People who belonged everywhere and nowhere at once. I enjoyed the mixed nationalities and how everyone easily merged and meshed despite where we came from. I quickly excelled as an instructor and moved from basic trainer to master instructor, where I was teaching instructors.

I had always known I was a teacher. When I was a little girl, I would set up all of my stuffed animals like children in my classroom, and I would teach them for hours and hours.

When that chapter ended, and I returned to the United States, the light went quiet for a moment. I was confused about what I wanted to do. I dabbled in hospitality, an obvious transition from the dive industry, but something in me knew immediately it was wrong. It didn't just fail to light me up. It felt like something was being drained from me. My light. My life.

Then I moved to Maui.

I found a house out on a beautiful bluff overlooking the Pacific Ocean. My neighbor had two horses. I was thrilled to be close to them again. After being separated from horses for years while I traveled, something in me exhaled. It felt like coming home. I told her I was going to find a job working with horses on the island. She furrowed her brow and told me that was highly unlikely.

I landed a job within two months.

The woman who hired me to ride her horses regularly brought in massage therapists and equine chiropractors to work on them. Something in me lit up immediately. I searched for training programs and found very little until I discovered an equine physiotherapy college based in England that offered the majority of the training online. I enrolled, and within about a year, I was an equine physiotherapist.

I moved to Colorado and built a practice. Then the healing work came. As I began to meditate daily and connect to my own energies, I started to easily connect to the energies of the horses.

I had some very profound experiences, like the Archangel Michael story. Then, I started to hear the thoughts of the animals. Honestly, at first, I didn't say anything to the owners. I didn't want them to think I was crazy. But some of it was simply too important not to share.

And when I did, it turned out to be incredibly useful. Sometimes it was information that seemed silly or unimportant to me, but when I shared it with the owner, their faces lit up in recognition, and they thanked me deeply. Before long, I opened my animal communication business. What had begun as a whisper between the horses and me had become its own practice.

And then one day, my Higher Self told me I would be working with humans instead of animals.

I didn't want to. I felt safe with the animals. Working with people felt unsafe. It felt exposing in a way that I wasn't sure I desired.

I resisted. But Creation didn't wait for my comfort. From that point forward, every single animal communication session I took began delivering information not about the animal, but about the owner. It was unmistakable. Almost humorous in its insistence, but also embarrassing. These people had hired me to hear about their animals, and everything I was seeing had nothing to do with their animals and everything to do with them.

My Genius was redirecting me, and it wasn't asking permission. I had no choice but to surrender. Very quickly, I shifted.

And that is when the wisdom truly began to move through me. That is when I felt myself aligning with something I couldn't fully name yet but recognized completely. It felt like the light was finally moving through clearer glass.

A high-profile friend invited me to speak on his astrology platform. I would show up weekly without a topic or any idea what I was going to say, and something would always come through. Not just words. Wisdom.

People would tell me the wisdom I was channeling had names, traditions, lineages. I hadn't studied any of them. All I knew was that it felt natural. Like remembering something I had always known.

The writing and speaking came next. I began to see visions of myself on stage. And though I had always been a writer, filling notebooks with fiction and poetry as a child, told by my Nana at age ten that I would write a book one day, I had become so disconnected from that part of myself over the years that I genuinely believed I was a horrible writer.

The people around me began saying, "You should write a book." That was 2019. This book was born in 2026.

It took that long because I had to live the wisdom I was channeling first.

Looking back, I can see that my Genius was present in every single chapter. The horses taught me about subtle energy fields and the intelligence of living creatures. The diving taught me presence, breath, and the power of surrendering to something vast. The healing work taught me the language of the body and the structures beneath the surface. The animal communication cracked open my intuition and my channeling. And the writing, the writing was always there, waiting patiently for me to stop believing the lie that I had lost it.

I was never without my Genius. I was always moving through it. The light was always present. The glass was simply clearing, one layer at a time.

This is what the journey to your Genius looks like. Not a straight line. Not a single revelation. A spiral. A labyrinth. A series of yeses to what lights you up, even when the destination is invisible, even when the road makes no sense to anyone watching, even when you yourself cannot see where it leads.

And this is available to you. Not someday. Not once you have figured it out. Now. Exactly as you are, with the signal that is already alive in you.

The direct path to your Genius is through your bliss. Bliss is not the same thing as enjoyment. We can enjoy many things. Bliss is the signal from your Soul. It is the resonance of your Incarnation Blueprint recognizing itself. When something lights you up at a cellular level, that is your Genius pointing the way home.

Follow What Ignites You

And here is the practice. Simply this:

Notice what ignites you. Not what makes sense. Not what is practical or logical or approved of by the people around you. What ignites you? What makes your body vibrate in resonance? What you return to again and again, even when you try to walk away from it.

Say yes to that. Even when it is small. Even when it seems irrelevant. Even when you cannot see how it connects to anything. The connection will reveal itself. It always does.

And notice what dims you. What drains the light? What you do from obligation, from social pressure, from the conditioning that says this is what responsible people do. The dimming is data. It is telling you that you have moved away from your signal.

Often, that signal has been replaced by someone else's.

Following someone else's signal causes us to forgo our own happiness for the benefit of others. But it doesn't actually serve them either. We tell ourselves that we are being kind, responsible, selfless. But living from obligation, from the need to keep others comfortable, from the fear of disappointing, that is not generosity. It is self-abandonment wearing the costume of care. And a person who has abandoned themselves has very little that is truly alive to offer anyone else.

When you follow what ignites you, your field emanates that Aliveness. It is not contained. It touches every person you come into contact with. It is a fire that ignites the fire within others. Saying yes to your own bliss is saying yes to a world of bliss. The most generous thing you can do is live from the truth of what lights you up.

Every time you say yes to what ignites you, you clear the glass slightly. Every time you say yes to what dims you, you cloud it. It is quiet and cumulative. And over time, the accumulation of your choices either reveals your Genius or obscures it.

Your Genius will not make sense to your human mind. It is not practical or even logical. Your mind is like a computer. It has been programmed with what is acceptable in our society. It doesn't think about your heart's desires. It thinks about the logical path to keep you safe.

Playing it safe will only ever feel dull and unfulfilling. Following your Genius isn't about taking enormous risks. It is about refusing to let logic be the gatekeeper of your aliveness.

But you are safe. You have always been safe. The version of you that needed to play it safe was protecting something that no longer needs protecting. And playing it safe will only ever feel dull and unfulfilling. Following your Genius isn't about taking enormous risks. It is about refusing to let logic be the gatekeeper of your Aliveness.

You don't have to make one enormous leap. You don't have to quit your job tomorrow or burn your life down. You begin where you are. You say yes to the small ignitions. You follow the breadcrumb trail with curiosity rather than urgency. You trust that the light knows where it is going, even when you don't.

And you meet the resistance, the fear, the failure with wholeness. And Aliveness awakens on the path of your Genius.

When confusion arises, when the path disappears, and the mind scrambles for certainty, know that this too is part of it. Creation is communion with the unknown. The mind wants to understand, to map, to arrive. But there are things that cannot be conceptualized. They can only be revealed. And they reveal themselves only to the one who keeps walking.

Just like a labyrinth, you can often appear to be moving away from the center when, in all actuality, you are moving closer. The path to your Genius is far from linear. As the labyrinth wraps around itself, it can often feel like the last leg is taking you all the way out to the furthest edge, before it wraps you directly into the center.

Fulfillment is not found at the end of what you do or accomplish. When you arrive at something, there will always be a next. Fulfillment lives in every moment that you are embodied in your Genius. It is not subject to outcomes or plans. When you are creating from your Genius, the outcome matters less than the truth of what is moving through you. You allow your life to flow because you are already fulfilled. Already whole. Already home.

Continue to trust, always, in what lights you up. Continue to take courageous action toward that bliss, and you will move through the labyrinth of life into the juicy center that is your Genius.

And the tools are already in your hands.

As you deepen your relationship to the Trinity of Creation, the Four Keys of Embodiment, and the Three Creator Centers, your genius will blossom, petal by beautiful petal.

It is not a destination; it is the journey. Relish it. Slow down enough to smell the aroma of life. Yet move quickly and nibble as the Spiritual Kung Fu master. Above all else, grant yourself the power of presence in this moment. The only moment. And allow all to reveal itself to you.

As you. Worthy. Sovereign. Alive.

CLOSING

I see you. I see your courage and your commitment. I feel your breath and your devotion. This work will ask everything of you and grant you more. It is no small feat that you land here on these words today.

And in the moments that you desire to give up, the I AM will beckon you home. It awaits, always, like a faithful lover. The lover of your lifetime. The communion with Creation. It is always there. It can never not be there. It can never abandon you or forget you.

That remembrance can grant you the freedom to surrender, breathe, and allow the process of awakening your Aliveness to unfold. Petal by petal.

All that you have learned are the tools that will grant you the power of each moment. Not something that bypasses it. Denies it. Or tries to speed it up for a quick fix. Tools that ground you deeper into all of it. Because the depth is where the intimacy is. The depth is what you crave. Not the end result. Not some superficial plaque to hang on your wall. Actual unification.

Each moment you move through the challenge, each time you choose wholeness over separation, you will emerge. More alive. More worthy. More sovereign. More of your Unique Genius shining brightly for the world to witness. Your light illuminating humanity. Illuminating the wounds of separation. A mirror of the I AM walking on the Earth.

With all of my love and devotion,

Alara Sage

GLOSSARY

The Four Keys of Embodiment

The four practices through which the body is fully inhabited and becomes a clear instrument of creation: Presence, Breath, Expression, and Movement. Each key works independently and powerfully. Together, they create conditions for the I AM to be held, sustained, and expressed through the body while meeting what arises. They are not a linear sequence to climb but a toolkit to reach for as the body calls.

Action

The third pillar of Coherent Creation. The expression of the Masculine. Movement that arises from clarity, inner sovereignty, and the I AM state. Not from lack, fear, or performance. Action in Coherent Creation is the arrow released: precise, committed, and surrendered to the intelligence of what has been set in motion.

Action Ignited

Taking action that arises from Core Desire and the I AM state rather than from performance, fear, or the need to prove. The quality of action in Coherent Creation. The arrow released with the full force of the bow, then surrendered.

Actualization

The process by which a desire moves from potential into physical form through Coherent Creation. Distinct from manifestation, which carries connotations of ego-based force, attempting to generate reality through will-power or visualization from a state of lack. In Coherent Creation, actualization is not a doing but an allowing. The I AM declares what is already true at the causal level, and reality reorganizes around that truth.

Aliveness

The felt sense of communion, and ultimately unification, with Creation itself. Not an emotion. Not a peak experience. The light of God, the I AM state, shining through every cell, every photon, every atom of your being. Aliveness is not generated. It is what becomes available when the wound of separation is met from wholeness. It is where duality meets itself, where the wound merges, and where God is realized as felt truth.

Awareness

The first pillar of Coherent Creation. The expression of the Child within the Trinity. The capacity to witness oneself and one's reality from acceptance and innocence, without judgment or agenda. Awareness sees the House of Mirrors clearly: the patterns, the projections, the wounds, without collapsing into them or needing them to be different. Distinct from Presence, which meets. Awareness sees.

Bliss

The signal from the Soul. The resonance of the Incarnation Blueprint recognizing itself. Distinct from enjoyment or pleasure, bliss is the body's recognition of its own truth. A navigational signal, not a reward.

The Child

The neutral principle within form. The coherence that holds the polarity of Masculine and Feminine without collapsing into either. Its defining gift is acceptance, the ability to meet what arises from innocence rather than an agenda. Expressed through the Heart Creator Center. The Child is the most available human bridge to the I AM state. Distinct from the inner child in psychological healing work. The Child here is a cosmic principle, ancient and eternal, not a developmental stage. The Child does not own changelessness; that belongs to the I AM. The Child is acceptance and innocence within form.

Circuitry Reprogramming

The practice of releasing all structure and allowing authentic expression to flow through the voice in the present moment—toning, humming, sounding, riffing—without agenda or performance. Channels wisdom, activates Aliveness, and reprograms the energetic circuitry of the body through the intelligence of spontaneous sound.

Circular Breathing

A continuous breath with no pause between inhalation and exhalation. Creates a loop of energy that builds momentum and moves what stillness cannot. Used to sustain the I AM state while meeting what arises in the body.

Coherent Creation

The act of creating reality from wholeness, with all aspects of Self in alignment. The I AM is anchored. The desire is known. The body is met. The action is sovereign. In Coherent Creation, you are not trying to get something you do not have. You are declaring what is already true at the causal level and allowing reality to reorganize around that truth. Neither manifestation nor healing. A remembering of what already is and allowing it to actualize into physical form. This is the art this book teaches.

The Complete Breath

A three-stage breath activating the belly, ribs, and chest simultaneously. Stimulates the vagus nerve, digestive, immune, and endocrine systems. The foundation breath practice of Embodiment. The breath that trains the instrument to hold the full capacity of the I AM.

Core Desire / Soul Desire

The deep, underlying desire beneath surface wants. The Soul's precise navigation system pointing to what needs to be met and integrated. Core Desires are not random. They point exactly to where the wound of separation is most entrenched and what the Soul most longs to unify. The hardest desires to create are often the most sacred: they point to the most solidified identity with separation and carry the most potential for Aliveness.

The Cosmic Womb

The void. Pure potentiality. The no-thing from which all creation is born. The physical womb is a direct container connected to the Cosmic Womb, which is why the feminine creative force is not metaphorical but literal in its power to bring forth form.

Creative Injection

Deliberately feeding the Third Eye with new experiences, perspectives, environments, art, and information to nourish vision and activate Genius. The practice of keeping the masculine creative center alive and responsive rather than calcified in the familiar.

Creator Consciousness

The state of recognizing and living as the I AM, as a direct fractal of Creation itself. A lived reality in which the self knows itself as the source of its experience rather than its victim.

Decree, Declare, Command (DDC)

A voice practice of speaking from the I AM state. Not affirmation. Not attempting to convince the mind of something it doesn't believe. DDC is the orchestration of creative energy from within into harmonic expression. It declares what is already true at the causal level. Spoken from wholeness, it lands in the body as recognition rather than aspiration.

Desire

The seed of creation. The Soul's compass back to wholeness and the I AM. Every desire, at its root, is the Soul's longing to come home to unification. Desires are not about the external reality. They are fundamentally about internal unification. Physical reality cannot grant what only wholeness can.

Divine Orchestration

The intelligence of Creation organizing circumstances in alignment with the I AM state and sovereign action. The precise response of a universe that is fundamentally coherent. Distinct from magical thinking: Divine Orchestration follows sovereign declaration and embodied action, not wishful waiting.

Divine Union

The union of Shakti (the rising feminine creative life force) with Shiva (the masculine principle at the crown). The inner unification of the Feminine and Masculine within the self that precedes and creates any outer union. Divine Union is the fruition of the Trinity working in coherence. Not a destination but a state that becomes increasingly available as the wound of separation is met.

Ecstatic Creation

The advanced expression of creation that becomes available once Coherent Creation is fully embodied. Here, the self no longer creates toward wholeness. It creates from it. Surrender is not a practice but a natural state. The creative life force moves through without obstruction. All Three Creator Centers merge into one unified field. The self has stopped chasing, fighting, or doing in order to get. This is the territory of the companion book, Living Aliveness: The Rapture of Ecstatic Creation, and is seeded but not fully taught in this volume.

Embodiment

The second pillar of Coherent Creation. The expression of the Feminine. Total availability to feeling, sensation, and the intelligence of the body. The body is the most sophisticated receiver available. It holds every memory, every wound, and every piece of wisdom the Soul has gathered. When fully inhabited through the

Four Keys of Embodiment, it becomes the primary instrument of creation.

Expression / Key #3

How the Soul sings vibration into life. Through voice, body language, clothing, words, and creative acts. Expression is the primary practice of declaring the I AM into the world. Distinct from performance, which expresses from lack. Sovereign expression arises from wholeness and carries the frequency of the I AM into the field.

The Feminine / The Mother / The Great Mother

The dark, the void, the infinite creative potential from which all form emerges. The magnetic, receptive essence. Governs feeling, embodiment, and the emotional body. Expressed through the Sacral Creator Center. The Feminine is not passivity but power, the deepest creative force in existence. As Great Mother, she is the cosmic scale of this principle: the Earth, the soil, the rising nourishment of Shakti through the body.

Fragmented Creation

Creating reality from the wound of separation. The ego, identified with not enough, declares separation without knowing it and receives it back faithfully as lived experience. Fragmented Creation is the natural result of a self that does not yet know its own wholeness. The wound runs the show, shaping choices, relationships, finances, and health, while the deeper truth of the I AM remains obscured beneath it. The outer world reflects the inner declaration with precision. Fragmented Creation does not stop until the identity beneath it is met.

The Golden Nugget

The precise wisdom that arrives through awareness. What could not be thought or analyzed into existence. The light held inside every shadow. The gift that lives inside every wound, every challenge, every House of Mirrors reflection, available only to the one willing to meet it rather than flee from it.

The Great Causal Body / The I AM

The outermost and largest of the bodies, containing all others. Pure existence. The source of creation at the level where all potentials are already fulfilled. The I AM operates from the Great Causal Body, which is why declaration at this level creates reality rather than affirming it.

Healing Trap

The subtle ego mechanism of approaching one's wounds through the lens of something being wrong. Attempting to fix, change, or transcend the self from a foundation of not enough only reinforces that very identity. The healing trap is the road of trying to get rid of what must instead be met. This book was born from the author's own years of walking that road.

The Heart Center

The Child Creator Center and the command center of creation. Governs the Soul blueprint, coherence, and union. The electromagnetic center of the body. The most powerful generator of the field to which creation responds. It is through the Heart that Soul retrieval occurs and Core Desires are revealed. The I AM declaration of the Heart Center: I am innocence.

The House of Mirrors

Physical reality as a reflective system. Every pattern, circumstance, relationship, and recurring experience reflecting the beliefs and identity structures creating them. The House of Mirrors is precision. It shows exactly where the I AM is being obscured by the wound of separation, and therefore exactly where the invitation to wholeness lives.

The I AM

The Great Causal Body. Pure existence, consciousness, beingness. The ground from which all of Creation arises. Not part of the Trinity of Creation. It creates the Trinity. Changeless. Boundless. The truth beneath every identity, every wound, every experience. The I AM contains every desire, every expression, every timeline in its already-fulfilled state. When declared from the body, as somatic truth, it operates at the causal level, where all creation originates. It cannot abandon you. It cannot forget you. It is what you are.

The I AM Practice

The foundational somatic declaration exercise in this book. Speaking "I AM" and allowing the body to activate and receive the truth of that state. As a causal-level declaration. The practice of training the instrument to hold the I AM while meeting what arises.

Incarnation Blueprint

The specific architecture of a Soul's current incarnation. Contains the gifts, lessons, desires, and unique structure through which Genius expresses in this lifetime. The Incarnation Blueprint is the fractal through which the self expresses. Bliss is the signal of the Blueprint recognizing itself.

The Indigo Body

The body the Soul returns to at death. Referenced in the author's direct experience of energetic work with clients and in the Shakti chapter. The Indigo body holds the Soul's continuity across incarnations.

Karma

Separation desiring to be met. Soul fragments frozen in unprocessed moments, awaiting unification. The Soul circling back—across lifetimes if necessary—to what still holds part of it entrapped in the wound of separation. Karma is not punishment. It is the intelligence of Oneness seeking to include what was excluded.

Kundalini

The coiled serpent. Shakti in her dormant, potential state at the seat of the Sacral Center, awaiting awakening. The coil is not inertia but containment: pure creative potential held at the root, ready to rise.

Kundalini Awakening

The activation of the coiled Kundalini energy initiates Shakti's rise through the body toward the crown. A Kundalini awakening can be catalytic and disorienting. It surfaces everything that obstructs Shakti's flow. Without the understanding and tools to meet what arises, it can feel like collapse rather than opening.

Manifestation

Used in this book to name the ego-based approach to creation, attempting to generate reality through force, visualization, or willpower from a state of lack. Distinct from actualization, which arises from wholeness. Manifestation, as commonly taught, reinforces the very separation it seeks to overcome by operating from the belief that what is desired is not already present at the causal level.

Martyrdom

The pattern of overgiving from the wound of not enough, depleting the self under the guise of care for others. Martyrdom is self-abandonment wearing the mask of virtue. It reinforces the identity of not enough by making the self's needs and desires secondary to everyone else's, and receives resentment rather than love in return.

The Masculine / The Father / The Great Father

The light, the spark, the precise directive intelligence that activates creative potential into form. Governs vision, focus, and discernment. Expressed through the Third Eye Creator Center. The Masculine is not domination but devotion. His highest expression is in service to the Feminine, providing the structure through which her creative potential becomes form. As the Great Father, he is the cosmic scale of this principle: the sun, the sky, the descending light of Higher Intelligence.

Movement / Key #4

Where Shakti meets the physical. The first act of creation, moving from within the body outward. In its feminine expression: no outcome, no destination, only the free flow of allowance. Movement releases what breath and presence cannot, because it meets what is stored in the body at the tissue level, the frozen energy of unprocessed emotion and unmet experience.

The Mycelium (as metaphor)

The nervous system as the living connective tissue that extends the physical body into the subtle realms where the Trinity already exists. Like mycelium in the forest, the underground network through which intelligence, nourishment, and communication move. The nervous system is the mycelium of the inner world: the channel through which the Trinity communicates with the self and through which Shakti flows.

Non-Attachment

Not detachment or indifference. Not caring less. The state of allowance for what arises from the quality of actions taken. The energy of the Child—curious, open, unattached to outcome, while fully committed to the desire. The arrow released from the bow surrendered to the trajectory already set.

Not Enough

The core wound of separation. The identity that arises when the I AM state is forgotten and the self measures itself against an impossible standard of worthiness. A universal human experience of the veil of forgetting. The ground from which Fragmented Creation operates. The precise invitation, when met with the I AM, to remember wholeness.

Oneness

The realized state of unity with Creation. Where duality meets itself and separation merges. A felt truth.

The ground that was always there beneath every experience of separation, simply obscured.

Performance

The Masculine expressing from the wound of separation. Doing in order to get. Action taken from the belief of not enough, attempting to prove worth through output. The distortion of sovereign action. Performance exhausts because it is never complete. There is always another proof required.

The Physical Body

The densest form. The vessel through which Aliveness is lived and experienced. Not an obstacle to spiritual reality, but its most direct instrument. Everything is held in the body: every memory, every wound, every piece of wisdom the Soul has gathered across lifetimes. The body is the most sophisticated receiver available. When fully inhabited, all of that information becomes accessible.

Presence / Key #1

The bridge between the infinite self and the finite human structure. Living intelligence, not merely a physiological function, but the primary vehicle through which the I AM circulates through the body. The most immediately available instrument for awakening Aliveness. Where breath is withheld, Aliveness is withheld. Where breath is full, creation has room to move.

The Sacral Center

The feminine Creator Center. Governs sexual energy, creative life force (Shakti), and the emotional body. The seat of creative potential before it becomes anything. The womb, in women literally, in all humans energetically, is directly connected to the Cosmic Womb, the void from which all creation is born. The I AM declaration of the Sacral Center: I am the yearning.

The Seat of Shakti

Located just above the root chakra, at the center of the body. Where Shakti coils, waits, and stirs. The physical point where the Cosmic Womb connects to the body.

Shakti

The creative life force energy. The primordial Feminine within all humans, regardless of body or identity. Shakti is not something generated. She is what awakens through the journey of communion. She is not produced by practice but revealed as the obstructions to her flow are met and cleared. Her journey through the body is the journey of returning to Oneness. When Shakti flows through a regulated nervous system, she becomes the primary instrument of Ecstatic Creation.

Shakti Activation Practice

Fire breath combined with perineal lock (*mula bandha*) to stoke and invite Shakti's movement up through the body. A practice of invitation rather than force. Creating the conditions for Shakti to rise, not compelling her.

Soul Retrieval

The process by which frozen Soul fragments, trapped in unmet karma or unprocessed trauma, are met with forgiveness and integrated back into wholeness. Occurs through the Heart Center. Soul retrieval is not a shamanic technique reserved for specialists. It is what happens whenever the wound of separation is met from the I AM with genuine forgiveness.

Spaciousness

Granting presence to the moment without anything needing to happen. The art of being so fully here that creation has room to blossom. A teaching that deepens in Ecstatic Creation, the precursor to full surrender.

Spiritual Bypassing

Detachment from reality, the refusal to engage with the House of Mirrors. Using spiritual practice, elevated states, or a transcendent perspective to avoid meeting the wound of separation. Distinct from non-attachment, which is fully present to what arises without being collapsed by it. Spiritual bypassing delays the very meeting it appears to pursue.

Spiritual Kung Fu

The art of being so fully present that one is simultaneously relaxed and dynamic. Like a lion at rest, completely still, coiled with the capacity to move. The state that becomes available when all Four Keys combine: time slows, potentials are felt before they actualize, and the self chooses from the I AM rather than reacting from the wound.

The Subtle Body / Subtle Bodies

The energetic bodies beyond physical form through which Higher Intelligence moves and is received. The Third Eye reads subtle light. The information is carried in the energetic field. Shakti moves through the subtle bodies before actualizing in the physical. The vagus nerve is the physiological interface between the physical body and the subtle bodies.

The Third Eye Center

The masculine Creator Center and the architect of creation. Governs vision, projection, focus, and discernment. Bridges the finite human mind and universal intelligence. The Third Eye reads subtle light, the energetic information of the field that the physical eyes cannot perceive. Its distortion is worry: focus turned against itself. Its highest expression is a clear, devotional vision of service to the Feminine's desire. The I AM declaration of the Third Eye Center: I am the vision.

The Three Creator Centers

The Sacral Center (Feminine), the Heart Center (Child), and the Third Eye Center (Masculine). The Trinity of Creation expressed within the human body, the mechanism through which ethereal energy becomes physical reality. Each center has its own intelligence, its own I AM declaration, and its own role in the creative process. Together, they form the complete instrument of Coherent Creation.

The Three Creator Centers Practice

Breathing sequentially through the Sacral, Heart, and Third Eye Centers to activate the Trinity in harmony within the body. A practice of coherence. Aligning all three centers before creation, declaration, or action.

The Three Phases of Shakti

The journey of Shakti's awakening through three distinct phases. Exposure: the densest blocks surface as Shakti rises—emotions, traumas, wounds of this life, ancestral lineage, and past lives. Disorienting and intense, this phase is also the most precise invitation to meet the wound of separation. Communion: the densest layers have been met. Shakti flows with less resistance. Peace arrives. The self begins to see beyond its own patterns into the larger field of humanity. Existence: nothing left to achieve, nothing left to become. Energy flows continuously. Life becomes simple. This is where Ecstatic Creation lives.

The Three Point Focus

A presence practice using three simultaneous anchor points: Touch (body, the Feminine), Sight (focused, the Masculine), Sound (field, the Child). The convergence of the Trinity within the body, a fast-acting tool for entering presence from any state.

The Three Relationships to Desire

Reactive: pursuing desire from lack, chasing the external expression of an internal wound, creating more of the same. Repressive: denying desire from lack, telling oneself that what is truly wanted is not available or not deserved. Creation: meeting desire from wholeness, holding the I AM while meeting the separation the desire reveals. Only the third relationship actualizes.

The Trinity of Creation

The foundational structure through which creation moves in form: The Masculine (Father), the Feminine (Mother), and the Child. Three expressions of one unified creative intelligence. The Trinity is not a religious concept but a description of how creation itself is structured, polarity held in coherence. The I AM creates the Trinity rather than being part of it.

Unique Genius

The irreducible, unrepeatable frequency that is you. Not a skill set, not a profession, not even a passion, though passion may point toward it. A vibration of consciousness moving through the unique fractal of your Incarnation Blueprint. What moves through the clear glass of the vessel when the I AM is fully anchored and the obstructions have been cleared. Genius cannot be copied, competed with, or replicated. It cannot be comprehended by the mind. The more fully the I AM is anchored, the more purely Genius moves through—unfiltered by the identity structures that were never actually you.

The Vagus Nerve

The physiological key to superconsciousness and the ability to create in communion with Source. The tissue through which Shakti actualizes from potential into form, and through which Higher Self descends into the body. In its clearest state, the vagus nerve functions as an antenna. A receiver for the energies of the higher bodies, allowing for deep communion with Creation and the direct flow of creative intelligence through the body into form.

The Why / Therefore Exercise

A layered inquiry practice to locate Core Desire beneath surface wants. Each want is questioned—why do you want this, and therefore what does that reveal?—until the true Soul Desire is reached. The practice of following the thread of desire all the way home.

Worry

The distortion of focus. Focus turned against itself, locked on what is not desired, feeding it with attention and vibration until it solidifies into reality. Worry visualizes the feared outcome, triggers the body with it, and begins to vibrate in the exact energies it seeks to avoid. The invitation when worry arises is not to stop thinking but to redirect focus toward what is actually desired.

The Wound of Separation

The core human experience of having forgotten wholeness. The belief of not enough that arises when the I AM state is obscured by identity, conditioning, and unmet emotion. The wound of separation is the precise map back to what the Soul most desires to integrate. Every desire points to it. Every challenge reveals it. Meeting it from wholeness, rather than trying to heal or escape it, is the direct path of Coherent Creation.

Yearning

The Feminine's natural magnetism. The ache of the womb toward what it desires to create. The pure magnetic power of the Feminine calling creation toward her through the force of her longing. Yearning is not a wound to be healed but a creative force to be honored.

Acknowledgments

My Nana told me, very distinctly, when I was ten years old, that I would write a book one day. She called me her shining light. From the moment her words left her mouth, I knew they were true. They stayed with me my entire life, patient, certain, waiting.

She passed away before I could board the plane to see her one last time. I had booked the flight. She let go before I arrived. There are no words for that particular grief.

For many years, I imagined the book would be fiction. I never could have known it would be this. And I think of her often as I hold these pages, how she herself would have needed this book. How it might have found her in exactly the places she carried quietly. Completing it felt like an adieu. A nod across whatever distance separates us now. The prophecy, finally fulfilled. Nana, this one is for you.

To my parents, thank you for holding space for a daughter who never followed the conventional path or abided by most rules. That could not have been easy. And yet you were always there. Your love and support have held me in ways I am still discovering.

Danny. You saw this book the moment you met me. What you could not have known, what neither of us could have known, was how much the relationship itself would become part of the teaching.

Initially, we fought. A lot. Our magnetism was extraordinary, and it brought up everything in us that wasn't in alignment with what we were building. Many times, I wanted to bail. And every time, the Higher Self would smack me—a term I use for the moments when the universe puts me firmly back in my place—and send me back in to own my part of it. Because I genuinely did not believe it was me. It took time to see that clearly.

The process cost me my ego. And the part of myself that had always kept one foot out of the door. Danny named that. He told me I wasn't devoted. It stung. And then, immediately, I saw how right he was. How I had lived that way my entire life, present but not fully in. Meanwhile, he is the ride or die. He taught me what devotion actually looks like. What it asks of you. What it gives back.

He has believed in me without wavering. He has seen me fully and never looked away. Without him, this book would not exist.

To my boys, you remind me every day of the Child that lives within us all. Your love for me is intrinsic and unstoppable. I love you both more than I know how to say.

I believed most of my life that I didn't even want to be a mother. But then one day, Willie's Soul came knocking on my door. A Soul that I knew, that I adored, and there was only one answer. Yes. I was pregnant in a month.

Monty followed closely after. Destined just the same. Your existence lives within every single word of this book.

To my mentor, Sam, who saw me long before I saw myself. The moment he met me, he told me that I was an Ecstatic. As I sat there in a chair across from him, rippling in blissful waves, barely able to sit up straight. He was able to direct me when I had no direction.

He introduced me to Sri Anandamayi Ma, the late Hindu saint, who taught me, through connection with her photos and essence, the power of the Mother. From her, I connected to the Great Mother, who has held me in unconditional love through all of my messy creations.

To my clients, you were there through all of it. Every internal shift, and there were many: substantial, regular, and not always graceful or clear. You believed in me when my own clarity was still forming. You held up a mirror to me just as I held one up to you, and I learned as much through our relationship as I ever could have alone. Those who have been with me from the beginning hold the most intimate place in my heart. And every single person I have ever had the privilege of working with matters to me. This book was shaped by all of you.

And to the horses.

I cannot think of you without tears, and I will not pretend otherwise.

Prince came first. A Morgan/Mustang with a heart of gold and the patience of someone who had chosen this work. He was the perfect horse for a young girl who needed somewhere to put everything. I could go anywhere on him. Do anything. He was always there when I fell off, through the laughs, the cries, all of it. He held it all without question.

Then came the many horses I worked on as a physiotherapist. They were far more patient with me than I was with them. They taught me to listen before I understood what listening really meant.

And now a herd that I do not own, only visit. Hours spent in their company, held by my dear friend's generosity and by something I can only describe as telepathic communion. Entire conversations without a single word. I always leave exhausted, never wanting to go. They receive me in a way that is difficult to put into language. They always have.

You have taught me how to be a true partner. How to listen with the whole body. How to heal. Your love is beyond what words can hold, and I am grateful for every moment of it.

About the Author

Alara Sage is a creator and a changer, by blood, by bone, by design. She has never been able to be otherwise, and she has long since stopped trying. Unable to follow a singular path, let alone a conventional one, since the moment she took her first breath.

She does not anchor in any one place. A world traveler, a horse rider, a mother. Rooted not in geography but in the living practice of what she teaches. She allows creation to lead her, one moment at a time. Curiosity and wonder guiding the way.

At thirty-five, newly a mother, her Kundalini awakened. A new son, a new identity, a new reality, and an experience she describes as the single most chaotic of her life, and yet the most alive. It was the beginning of everything that this book contains.

She has lost it all and rebuilt from the ground up. Not quickly. Slowly, steadily, facing the separation within herself at every choice and every turning point. She has been a scuba diver, a rock climber, a horsewoman, always drawn to the edges where something vast opens, within and without. Always seeking the places where mastery meets surrender.

What this book required of her above all else was humility. The humility of dying and being reborn, over and over. The humility of thinking she knew who she was, and discovering she had no idea. And the courage, after years of embodying this teaching in the fire of her own life, to finally write it down.

For over fifteen years, Alara has worked with hundreds upon hundreds of people as a mentor, liberator, and multidimensional healer. She is a natural paradox holder, equally at home in the vast and the intimate, the cosmic and the cellular. A channeler and wisdom bearer who holds the container of the Mother in her work. An activator of Shakti in those ready to receive her.

Her work lives at the intersection of consciousness, creation, and the fire that burns between them. Creating, experiencing the process, and teaching others to do the same. That is the work. That has always been the work.

Awakening Aliveness is her first book. The second, Living Aliveness: The Rapture of Ecstatic Creation, is already alive and waiting to be written.

Alara is the founder of Ecstasia Academy—the school of power and creation—dedicated to supporting those ready to meet themselves in the moment and create from a place of Genius, sovereignty, and Aliveness.

To work with Alara or explore her offerings, visit alarasage.com or ecstasiaacademy.com